Between Proverbs and Poetry

A Collection of Poetry
by
Tywanda L. Howie

Thank You.

Tywanda L. Howie

Cover and Layout Design by:
Sarah Thompson, SWAK Design

Published by:
Victorious Books Publishing
Brandon, FL
Victorious Books is a trademark of Victorious Living International.

Tywanda's Headshot Photography by:
Geneva Fonda Photography™
www.genevafonda.com

Publisher's Cataloging-in-Publication data

Howie, Tywanda L.
Between proverbs and poetry : a collection of poetry on life, love and the
discovery of self / Tywanda L. Howie.
p. cm.
ISBN 978-0-9841815-4-4

1. Self-realization --Poetry. 2. Women --Conduct of life --Poetry.
3. Love poetry, American. I. Title.

PS3608.O95728 B49 2011
811/.6 –dc22
2011941014

Dedicated to my heavenly Father and the earthly mother and father you were gracious enough to bless my life with. Without you three, there would be no me.
I love you each --
indefinitely.

"It's human nature to feel, to search, to learn, to dream, and to believe. Between Proverbs and Poetry encompasses this nature from beginning to end. It is a journey through the human condition, and its candid point of view stimulates self-reflection. Readers will be captivated with each turning page, and upon completion of this "literary legacy"... Be inspired to LIVE. I will cherish this work of art for all my days."
- Stephanie Artist, Spoken Word Artist and Poet

"Tywanda Howie is gloriously gifted with the charm and fascination you see with great writers. Reading Between Proverbs and Poetry is akin to having a worthwhile conversation with an admired older relative. It transports the mind on a spiritual and poetic path scarcely travelled by many. It is impossible to read this book and not be humbled, enlightened, and transformed ... simply astonishing!"
- Edmund Okocha, Author and Poet

Between Proverbs and Poetry revived me when I received an advanced copy. This volume is full of captivating imagery that paints a portrait of an artist in motion, an artist on a journey. The poems are not random, spontaneous in subject, and positioning. Each piece is full of purpose and are chock full of variety. Between Proverbs and Poetry is a soulful piece of work. Ms. Tywanda Howie is telling her story."
- Desmond Polk, Editor-In-Chief at DessysInn

"When you're GREAT, you don't need to TELL people you're great. They already know."
- Ebony R. Wilmore, Author and Spoken Word Artist

Table of Contents

Table of Contents

CHAPTER SIX: I FOUND HIM

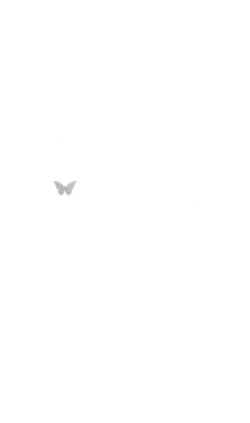

PAYING HOMAGE

There was both life and the purpose of life before you existed. Some thought, action or person that helped pave a path on a road you would one day be destined and willed to walk on. Before me, there was a Maya Angelou, a Nikki Giovanni, a Langston Hughes, a Robert Frost, a Walt Whitman amongst many others. Without them or their obedience in submitting to the divine purpose they were born to fulfill, my exposure to their work at an early, adolescent age and the initial igniting of my love for poetry may have never existed. This book may not have ever been written. My first poem may have never found rhyme. Without their influence, I don't believe I would have truly understood and appreciated the wisdom, the art, the mechanic or even the passion for poetry. If it were not for the art and process of poetry in its own right; the labor that goes behind the techniques, devices and rhyming patterns; the ability to see and express through one's third eye; or the intentionally inexplicable process of evoking emotion through the use of words, I do not know who I would be, where I would be or how I would have coped with the ebbs and flow of life. I owe poetry, its champions and its rich ancestry, the very ink that flows from my pen. May that ink be a thread that weaves us all together in one eclectic society of poets. No matter what road you decide to walk in life and wherever that path may take you, never forget to pay homage to your purpose and those who have walked in that light before you. I humbly take my first step into their likened footprints, hoping that one day, my work will be considered as equally moving, captivating, inspiring, unnerving and eloquent as those who came before me. This chapter pays homage to that passion, literary legacy and the writing process of poetry. I owe my aesthetic love for language to it.

Fearful
A Double Tetractys

I'm

afraid

that I won't

make this a means –

that poetry may not be my purpose.

Perhaps God gifted me a different way

that I don't know,

haven't found,

so *I'm*

scared.

Stream of Consciousness

I often run out of things to write;
Words to play
with or on.
I'm often left
with an inability to finish complete sentences
or thoughts --- that run on.
Yet,
I have a desire to make words breathe
effortlessly,
like water flowing
steadily, ---
down a stream of consciousness
leaking at the river's mouth,
dripping out,
pouring about,
Poetry.
Poetry that oozes from the lead
of my pen and fingertips.
'Til epiphanies 'bout life

strike like a meteor and hit
the cerebrals of my brain.
I'd be content as long as
language always remains.

I don't walk in iambic pentameters,
Don't dream of blank verse or stanzas.
I am not prose.

I quite easily transpose
my thoughts.
My soul's purpose is to scribe linguistic gospels
through words
from the figurative arrangement of verbs.
Yet subtle enough that you don't get it
when you're first hit with it,
but can't deny it
once you've tried it.
When all else fails
I know how to write it –
Life, that is.

Write Owl

Isn't life just pretty at night?
Images of pitch black skies
and the moons illuminating light.
I'm a night owl at heart,
My mind awakes in the dark,

It's something about the silence

Minus the riff raff and violence
that leaves a mark
on my mind,
sparks thought
through the nighttime.
And it thinks better
when it becomes in synch
to the chirping of crickets
and the majestic sounds heard of
nocturnal creatures who'd rather spend their days
sleeping and nights creeping about the earth.
I am awakened by the night.

I see the cadence in no light.
Promises seem attainable through sight.
Night vision -
Nocturnal transmissions
forcing me through life's transitions.
And I can't stop it,
it is quarter past two and I won't block this --
My mind is churning
with topics.
Topics that I need to talk about,
so I write them out.
And I think ... I know,
that when I'm left
to my own devices,
and time is priceless,
I would rather sleep 'til noon,
and wake up when the sun's
got less time on deck
than the moon.
'Cuz isn't life just pretty at night?
Images of pitch black skies
and the moon's illuminating light.
Yeah, life's sure pretty at night.

A Musing Weather
A Haiku

April's spring showers ---
water my pen to rhythm
harmoniously

So I Type

Blank canvas to write;
Empty notebook to plight
my insight about life.
So I type.

I type on keys of laptop
like Mozart
on a baby grand.
Effortlessly,
thoughts escape from me
and manifest themselves
in reality
with the stroke of my keys.

Blank canvas to write;
Empty notebook to plight
my insight about life.

So I type.

They say out of sight,
out of mind
So I type mine out
line by line
Therefore, my metaphors
are never caught in a bind
between verb and noun agreement.
Such a bereavement
cause to the pen and pad, as
the keyboard is its offspring and
the art form of penmanship,
its dad.

Blank canvas to write;
Empty notebook to plight
my insight about life.
So I type.

Purposeful Proverb

Scattered thoughts that swarm my mind like bees
'round a hive.
When I'm alone in peace is when I feel most alive.
Attention pulled into various directions, a mental
tug-of-war,
At times, I'm not quite sure
of my writing's purpose.
Resisting the monotony of habitual autonomy
quite cynical because on life, I didn't deserve this.
I aspire to be more than an inkblot on Earth's spot.
You can pull petals on a flower, but forget me not.
I want to transform that ink spot into a verbal
masterpiece;
that single-handedly could read strength to those
currently weak.
I don't want to just write for the mere sake of
writing.
I want my words to be my weapon, victoriously
fighting

to bring life to those mentally and spiritually dying.

I want to catapult them high, free from captivity.

I want to sprinkle pieces of my poetry 'round the world - call them my proclivity.

So that my words can fertilize Mother Nature's ground and can birth a literary emancipation to those mentally bound.

I aspire to be profound;

In both diction and penned transcript.

Writing is my therapeutic prescript.

I wish to be instilled with knowledge that churns 'round like a merry-go,

And come full circle so I would reap the wisdom that I desire to sow.

I envision college students dissecting my poetry in an attempt to understand the soliloquy.

My writings are nothing more than hieroglyphics interpreting me.

Can you interpret me?

Literary Linguini

Labeled a word nerd – lyrical junkie,

If linguistics be a teacher, I'm signed up to be her flunky

On a fit for a hit of the next fix of poetry,

A literary misfit, I trip off metaphor and analogy,

Yet equally, I'm moved by hyperboles and similes,

Verbal devices, techniques and styles are friends to me,

The antonym means it's my enemy.

My idols, a toss-up between Shakespeare, Hill and Angelou,

My free verse flows fluid like water in the bayou,

A sonnet for breakfast and for lunch, a haiku.

An epic for dinner and for fun – a pun,

A pet peeve for error in syntax and sentences that run.

My favorite writing motifs, without any doubt or hesitation,

Go to two lyrical heavyweights: personification and

alliteration.

And that symbol, four lines up, undoubtedly a Caesura pause,

Rhyme so right that the applause gets caught in a clause.

Iambic pentameter is the beat of mi Corazon,

From foreshadowing, symbolism, plot and tone.

My cerebral sends pulsating orgasms that leak through my pen,

And that allusion of climax sends it into spasms all over again.

I pack the power of prose in one lyrical wordplay,

Draft adjectives of distinct diction like my anecdote for a day.

A dictionary and thesaurus my crutch, a sacred text,

Long to leave each line a cliffhanger, yearning for what's next.

My daughter will be named Kyrielle and my son, Langston,

If poetry tried to leave me, I'd hold its stanzas up for ransom.

I want to be the Patti LaBelle of this poetry, with a hint of Marvin Gaye,

'Cuz violets are blue and roses red ... that's a little too cliché.

Editorials and loose compositions like a comforter blanket on my bed,
I am a word nerd, onomonopian sounds buzz inside my head.
A recovering verbal addict, yet writing is my therapy,
On the block waiting for a next hit -
With sign, "Will write for Poetry."

For The Love of Poetry

For the love of poetry I -
Endure sleepless nights
And less than mediocre writes.

For the love of poetry I -
Isolate myself from friends
Destined to make this a means to an end.

For the love of poetry I -
Think deeper than the average being's sea
Constantly challenge my thoughts and philosophies.

For the love of poetry I -
Swallow all of my fears and insecurity
To enable my words to revel in transparency

For the love of poetry I -
Decided to tattoo it on my brain

So the elements of it will always

:remain
Engrained ... in me
With the ability to sustain ... in me
For the love of poetry.

I Am Poetry

I am poetry.

I breathe prose.

Literary rhyme rests on the crest of my pillow,

From the walls of life, my writes echo,

Watch your step though.

Etchings of my linguistic sketching lay placidly at
your feet,

*Find me diverged on the path where
proverbs and poetry meet*

Resting atop a pile of language, sound asleep,

If you know poetry, well, I'm certain you're familiar
with me,

We flow compatibly --

down the same stream of consciousness,

It's quite coincidental that we possess identical
purpose,

And might I eloquently confess --

We're uncompromisingly inspiring!

To not know of us can be equated to the
commencement of dying.
'Cuz there's no denying our worth,
We leave leaflets of our metaphors that lurk --
sporadically 'round Planet Earth.
Find my heartbeat meandering the linear compounds of
my work.
I was birthed -
to expose the transparencies of human life,
Euphoria settles on the tip of the pen I use to write each
night,
I am quite a sight!
Yes, quite a sight to behold is me.
Because I breathe prose
And well, I am poetry.

My Rosetta Gem

On the spine of the Rosetta stone
I etched the enigma of my story.
Language transcends through time.
It breaks through all barrier lines.

Decipher me.
Poetry!
Unlock my hidden treasure.
Once a stone, now a diamond -
I've measured up against life's pressure.

On the spine of the Rosetta stone
I etched the anomaly of my story.

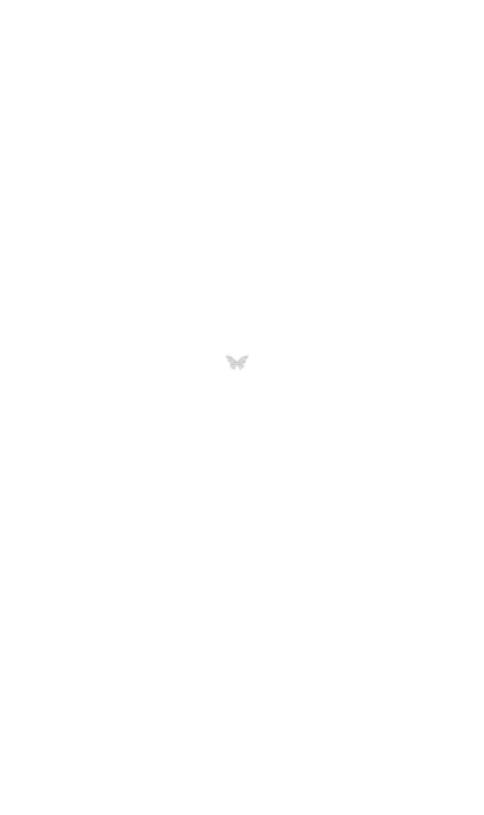

Chapter 2

TIP TOEING AROUND
WHITE ELEPHANTS

Some issues in life aren't the easiest to address, especially if they make you feel uncomfortable. Truthfully speaking, our nation was built on a herd of white elephants with an array of controversial topics we'd prefer not to speak about. It's glazed over lightly in the history books and swept under the rug to provide an illusion of good housekeeping. They are our ugly truths. The problem is, much like a wound, it won't ever heal properly until you thoroughly clean out the infection. You can't ever heal from something if you continue to trip over the same rug without a better understanding of why it's posing as a safe haven to the harsh realities of life in the first place. We tip-toe over a lot of secrets in life. Tip-toe over heartache. Tip-toe past transparency. Tip-toe around the skeletons in the closet. Tip-toe over truth in an attempt to not disturb those obvious white elephants in the room. Would someone just PLEASE address them!? Transparency can feel awkward. It can make you uneasy. You will shift in your seat. However, there is a guaranteed level of freedom and healing that directly follows being genuine and transparent. Make no apologies for who you are, where you come from and the things that helped construct you, whether those things are good, bad or fall somewhere in between the proverbs of life. This not only holds true to you as an individual but holds true to us as a greater society as a whole. So I say, point out that white elephant in the room, address it, make amends with it, and work collectively as a whole on getting it safely to the nearest safari – where it rightfully belongs.

Shattered Dreams
A Ballad

Do you know where shattered dreams go
when from kids' hopes they leak?
Off their pillows, out the window
while drifting fast to sleep.

One such dream was Martin King
he'd dream of freedom's taste,
Marched a movement for civil rights
was shot for goodness sake!

There was Rosa, on bus she sat
with tired spirit blue,
Arrested for doing what's right
birthed a movement that grew.

Do you know where shattered dreams go
when from kids' hopes they leak?
Off their pillow, out the window

while drifting fast to sleep.

For where did all the dreamers go
with purpose, goals in hand?
Realities of shattered dreams
that has drifted to some far land.

It seems as if change has occurred
no glimpse of hope in sight,
This era seems uneventful
in need of guiding light

Do you know where shattered dreams go
when from kids' hopes they leak?
Off their pillow, out the window
while drifting fast to sleep.

I Want Out

I want out of all these boxes
That is where I like to think,
I want out of all these labels
Systematic lemmings marching in sync.

I want out of all these boxes
Please don't circle, check or X,
I can't fit into a category
My being is too complex.

I want out of all these boxes
These systematic rules of thumb,
The classification and organization of life
Gone cause me to riot with gun.

I want out of all these boxes
Can't stand to be held bound,
I'm a rebel, terrorizing renegade

Step back or get knocked down.

I want out of all these boxes
Don't force me into your mold,
March to the beat of a different drum
Your failed attempts are getting old.

I want out of all these boxes
This hypnotizing guise that can transfix,
Took the blinders off of my state of being
No longer part of this matrix.

I want out of all these boxes
Set free from mental and spiritual captivity,
Once shackled and chained: I adorn no more
My God, Jehovah, has rescued me.

Technically Busy

Busy schedule

Busy life,

When do we have time

to enjoy the price ---

That we pay.

to live this way?

Busy schedule

Busy me,

I blame it all on

Technology.

Check your e-mail

Text your friend,

Carry your laptop

Work never ends.

They got me traced

by this electronic leash,

Check your cell

each time it beeps.

Got cake in the bank

can't enjoy its reap,
No couch; no sit
Stay quick on your feet.
Must educate more
to get ahead,
Graduate school
Means no time for bed.
Communicate much
Via e-mail and text,
Spending quality time
Happens less and less.
Or perhaps the ideal
Has become truly historic,
Next time the text comes
Try to ignore it.
Try writing a letter
or sending a real card,
Break real bread
Face time seems hard.
Busy schedule
Busy we,
I blame it all
on technology.
Make this meeting

give back to the kids,

*So much on my schedule
No time to love.*

Arise at five

to make the gym,

take the bus to the city

Autopilot: Repeat! Again.

Join this organization

Network with them,

Leave a mark on this nation

No time for him.

Write this paper

Research this thought,

Busy, busy, work bees

and if it for naught.

Busy schedule

Busy me,

I blame it all

on technology.

All work no play

is our motto,

Eggs in basket

Head on, full throttle.

Stretched so thin
Bend this way
inside this box
Careful what you say.
Multitask
or you won't last,
a balancing act
Wear many hats.
Find a speed bump
Please slow down!
There's more to life
than what is around.
There is world peace
Even poverty;
The health of others
Spirituality.
You could go green
Help Mother Earth,
Find you true purpose
Recognize your worth.
Busy schedule
Busy me
I blame it all
on pride and greed.

Corporate America

Enslaved to the system of commerce
willingly devoted as a sacrificial lamb
it is in an arena of scrutiny you stand,
a prisoner to Corporate America.
Voluntarily adorning a merry cuff
of imprisonment 'round your hands
The product of a dream to own
more than a mule and some 40-acred land.
With a degree in hand,
Blinded by the luminous imagination of
money, power and respect.
Supporting the weight of the glass ceiling
that sits on your shoulders; nape of neck.
Vowing to not get embrangled into its system
Finding yourself thrown under buses
Mastering the art of politicking
Consider it the new age religion.
Aspiring to be the Chief
ruling the Indians in your division.

Corporate America isn't forgiving.

The initiation into a sentence of drudgery,

I'm certain, is tough

yet, we all desire to work in it; it's a merry cuff.

You toil ten to twelve hours a day

for less than a dishonest man's pay

No overtime; promotions, slow over time

Tap dancing for some estranged man

Whose eating diamonds while you sift through sand

That plays putt-putt on some green with Uncle Sam.

Corporate America is a systematic jam.

'Cuz the bills need paying

In need of health care benefits, so you staying

inside the prison walls of a deck of cards

that one day gone fall.

Protected by entrepreneur's law

and when they pink-slip and right-size

Check the deception in its eyes

Individual before corporation, for naught

Biweekly you contractually agree to swallow lies.

Nothing more than an arbitrary number

Stick your neck out while avoid making blunders

Corpse-raped, corporation

Suck you dry like grape to raisin

The labor force, its players and stage
Oh, the joys of minimum wage
Check your 401Ks, got pension these days?
From Baby Boomers to Generations X and Y
An automatic robot; you just trying to get by
Took the gig to fuel your dreams of a good life
Dreams not birthed left you with stress and strife
Walk that tight rope, juggle that act
Profit the bottom line or out comes the axe
How much longer you going to play the fool?
Tried to get ahead, you retreat back to school
It isn't what you do, it's who you know
More on what you reap, less on how you sowed
All aboard the bandwagon: Get right, or get left
Selling souls to get that tax-deducted paycheck
After you pay Paul, tell me, what's left?
Bound by the vicious cycle that practices theft
A fraudulent smile disguises your internal resentment
Of the firm that robbed your life
And left you entrenched in
'Til you pull the curtains, and disclaim you've had
enough
Back to work, put on your merry cuffs.

Passing Pass Love

You are looking for her.
Looking for her in shades of white-is-right light skin.
Looking for her in light eyes and unethnical butt and
thighs,
Looking for her in perched pinkies and snouted nose,
from atop a gated community with a condescending
air and pose.
Looking for her in straight-and-long-is-never-wrong-
type hair.

I get there.
Watch and stare,

As with a strong-willed desire and despair,
You attempt to uncover love based off how her brown
paper bag test may fare.

I am looking for him.
Looking for him who has chocolate hands,
And a Mandingo, statuesque stand.

Looking for him to pound proud and protruding chest
In an attempt to confess he is the King of the Jungle,
I am looking for he who is neither meek nor humble.
Black, strong and debonair with calloused hands,
He is my dreamt definition of an authentic black man,
I am in awe of his build, workmanship and ability to
command.

In our searching, we don't see each other.

*Our eyes cause ears to mute out the sync
of like heartbeats,*

We are too proud to realize that destiny
May have willed caramel and mahogany to meet.
There is too much melanin in my color.
My natural is a little too kinky,
The cellulite 'round my stomach and thighs, a lil' too
wrinkly;
Than you'd prefer it to be.
And I am dismayed at the lack of melanin in yours.
Your berries not sweet enough.
Your black blushes pink,
Your thinned lips make me think
That your mental speak may be a bit too white-washed
for me.

We're passing - *literally*,

Passing passed love

Based off a skewed psychological fallacy of what we

see.

When love should bleed red, pass skin deep

And not liken a visual hypocrisy

Of what others proclaimed the effects of slavery to be.

Your momma told you to breed pretty.

Kept your skin, kept from too much sun and inner cities.

Left you searching for topaz amid a tarred city.

And I was told that black was beautiful.

Literally, so I says beauty within me.

But what if we...

What if God entrusted the key to your heart in the hands

of this chocolate girl?

And what if Mr. Light was meant to be right in my brown

world?

Can you move pass social caste and cultural dogmatic

idolatries

To spot love?

For isn't love found in the sound of a blaring, bursting

heartbeat

Deep beneath porcelain skin and what onyxes eyes may
see?

We're passing,

Wasting time passing passed what we feel --

Cosmic connection.

Mental erection.

Spiritual progression.

All because we can't get over a reflection

Of what we were told *love should see-like.*

Flipped Upside Down

They call it the circle of life,

I call it the circle of strife!

Give a dog a bone,

Let that dog alone.

Hookers and whores

the streets want more of you,

to prostitute the good out of you.

Drugs on streets

Careful when you speak

No snitching,

More twitching --

Numb mouths

And empty stomachs.

I can't stomach

The state of my people

And the state of our homes,

Momma working three jobs

Means momma leaving them alone.

So the streets become their village
That's left to raise her child,
Stress build up after 'while
So teen boy start tokin' Black & Milds;
That eventually feed into weed,

If only momma knew what was happening to her seed.

And teen she, she start popping E pills,
'Cuz her girlfriends told her she should feel
What it feels like to be a woman;
Even though her clothes aren't filled to feel what a
woman should.
She prematurely has been deflowered into womanhood.
Holey socks and tattered feet
that beat those streets,
While totting that heat
And ducking for cover,
My young brother
Who only knows his mother
through her multiple lovers.
Cops run streets as bums or buyers undercover
Trying to uncover why he's

Too scared to lead his tithe,

Loose, wide-hipped women

Reppin' the title of baby momma 'stead of bride,

Just trying to discover love's who, what, when and why.

And this has become the mentality of many

And the aggravation of few,

Such a perpetuated vicious cycle

Talented tenth, what are we to do?

Call in the mentally acute and spiritually gifted

The urban streets are in need of a revolutionized rescue.

All must become educated!

Bridging the gap is a needed measure

'Cuz instead of knowing how to mathematically measure

Wet and dry weight,

Why don't we debate

About the sake

of your mind?

'Cuz it's a terrible thing to waste

and it's been replaced

by drug lords, liquor stores, poverty and whores.

You keep following the pack

And the system, prison or dead is what's in store,

Tell the world you want more!

Tattoo it on your mind, and demand it,

Tell the government you can't stand it,

Tell the people the health care, education and housing

system are broken

And you want it Neosporined up and bandaged.

So you can become black pearls 'stead of lumps of
coals,

So you can progress into royalty and have dreams and
goals

'Cuz something has fueled this habitual nightmare,

Mind so polluted you can't see the stars in the night's
air.

If only you could find from within yourself

A river of flowing water that lies right there

Open up a book, and you've just unlocked your mind,

If men are walking on the moon, these streets shouldn't
define

You or limit your capacity

There are no fences or cages, so let loose from the
captivity,

Flipped upside down

This world is upside down

Flipped upside down

This world is upside down

So what are you going to do?

One-Third Are Missing

One-third are missing

And I miss them

suppose to be our future husbands

My Nubian king

Black men

Stuck in prison.

Imprisoned

By this crooked system.

Estranged men

to a free society

I highly recommend

we find a better way

to reprimand and rehabilitate

than prison.

Behind bars

Folks are still killing and hustling

And who you think getting them drugs in?

And if and when he does get out

It's still messed up

His trust in

Politics that are corrupt.

He's bankrupt.

No snitching

He won't fess up.

Bad luck

Recession now

Job rate foul

less chance for Jim Crow now.

End of the stick, short -- how?

Can you follow it?

This system been 'round

to swallow it ---

Swallows them up in a black hole,
a lion behind black poles.

Labeled a black mole.

And just like them –

Where the natural niche is a safari,

the natural niche to my black men is

Head of his family

but when the last time

you stepped in that?
Momma head of the household
according to the facts.
Imagine that.

One-third of them are missing, black
Got us single, educated black women
tripping, black
My options are slim and slipping, black
My husband's dead or stuck in prison.

And this isn't to say some haven't done wrong,
But a large part of this urban genocide
I attribute to slavery gone wrong.
And isn't that ironic?
Racial supremacy is iconic -- to them
But what about my children?
They suppose to be
Black diamonds and pearls.
If I ruled the world.
But, you can't demand him
to right his wrong
When you got the heel of your boot
on the nape of his neck
I suspect

It's you massa that has done wrong.

Always trying to oppress folks

to get them to play along.

Drink the juice you've made,

and sing your version of the same song.

They will never fit into a society

That they were smuggled in

On the same boats of the drugs

You govern the smuggling in.

White-collar crimes

Got the worker bees doing the time.

Truth be told, they're just copying;

you smuggle humans, they smuggle drugs

Isn't it all a win-win?

Ask Enron and them.

Diaspora

You asked for it!

So quick -

To mask your sins

but expose the affects of it.

Yes, you're truly the real drug lords.

But, instead of crack,

you smuggled the backs

of my ancestors as slaves.

To you, be all the praise?

Right, Mr. Columbus?

For three centuries of 365 days.

And you wonder why

Black athletes amaze.

You took the toughest and the biggest

to enslave.

Been knocked off their throne

Africa is home

Ode to my black men.

For one-third of them is missing

Locked up in this prison system.

And I'm sorry Martin Luther King

Don't really know if we can sing

Free at last

Free at last

Cuz since the shackles came off

The black-men-in-prison rate

Has surpassed

Our expectations

They profiting off my husband's fate – and

Can't even ride down the street

Racial profiling replaces

Picnics of the finest meat

Read your history, or you might sleep --

On that last line.

So, I'll repeat.
Racial profiling replaces
Picnics of the finest meat.
So I say BBQ's instead.
Oh, what a feast!
Of strange fruit dangling from trees.
Prisons replace graves of my peeps
Reparations, please?
How you going to repay
A King that you renamed a coon.
A Queen that you turned into a whore
Obsessed with her curves and body;
that's all my sistas are exploited for?
The traces of DNA that live
along the Atlantic Ocean floor.
And you wonder where the aggression
comes from,
you try stripping a man from his family
and his internal freedom,
Lock him down
When he use to running a kingdom.
That notion is absurd.
All lies, the truth still goes unheard.
It's our fault, we're too lazy to open a book
Got my peoples all up in the news.

Got me singing the blues.

While you own the rhythm,

but I own this pen.

So while I write this plight

I'll keep sending my kites

to my husband at night.

Reach for the stars.

Ain't no Jupiter and Mars

from behind prison's walls.

Ain't no Jupiter and Mars

from behind prison's walls.

Victim of Self

So I tell him often,
don't speak about it,
be about it
because actions speak
Louder than words
you can spit 16 bars
and accomplish nothing
they still just words.
It's still just a verse.
It's the fear of doing
that's truly your curse.
And you can rehearse
in your mind
Over and over again
your action plans
the talents in your hands
but scared is he
to make a move
got dreams of making it big

MTV cribs

Top story on Actions News.

Don't two-step yet--

He lacks rhythm

He got the blues.

So, that's the story that he sings

His hopes drowned out

By such an eerie ring

Of unbirthed dreams

That he's abused

Nothing new, he's all used

In need of a muse

Talents galore

Too afraid of what's in store

Caught in the red zone

Anguish, he calls his home.

It's the fear of the unknown

Got him in a chokehold

Simple thoughts of succeeding,

Fear stops his tracks cold

He's glued to the seat

Of self-torture, self-defeat

Isn't others he's trying to beat?

That'd be a win-win.

But, the hardest is him
He's his own competition.

Inflictions of the mind and self
starting from within.
The devil has been plotting on him.
Gripped by insecurities
Covered up by male infidelities
Looks can deceive
from the naked eye.
Outward, he so fly
on the inside ---
Oh my.
Mental affliction,
Depression he's battling
Washed up on some shore
don't know what his purpose is for.
Lonely and weary nights
Coupled by self hate
Fear of succeeding,
Crippling his blessed fate
so he's lost somewhere between
the bottom of self-pity where
He rests his head
and the dreams of his own mansion

and a king size bed.

If he could only kill himself ---
figuratively
He'd survive --- literally.

Cuz he's his worst nightmare
Look in the mirror and stare
And I pray for him nightly
Wish he'd open his eyes and see
what I've been seeing all along.
He's a victim of himself
Missing the lines of freedom's song.

A Modern Day Revolt

Does my liberation offend you?
Now that I've aspired to unmask myself
Does my freedom unnerve you?
Now that I have a sense of duty, pride and wealth

Does my confidence cause resentment?
Now that my head is held high
Does my self-worth lessen your contentment?
Now that you sense esteem in my third eye

Does my independence provoke you?
Now that I live, learn, love and am elated.
Does my nonconformity imprison you?
Now that I've become emancipated

Does my intellect cause a level of dissent?
Now that I have access to your blue sky
Does my generational gift present torment?
Now that you see my red blood won't dry.

The Measurements of Success

A Naani

Success isn't measured
in monetary increments you receive

but in *heartbeats*

of love you give.

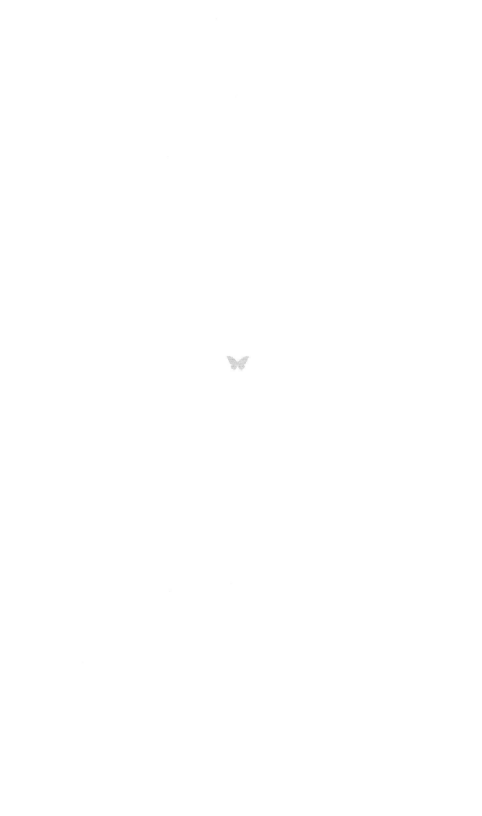

Chapter 3

NOSTALGIA

Can we take a trip back? A trip back to a place where life was easy. Let's try an exercise in mental clarity and reminiscing. Do me a favor. Lie across your bed in complete darkness and silence, then close your eyes. Take a deep breath. Let your mind drift, race and explore down memory lane. The moment you catch a glimpse of a memory or thought that brings a smirk, a smile or warmth to your face - that is nostalgia. It is a tingle. A feeling. A sense. Remembering the taste of your favorite dish. The feeling you felt when hearing your favorite song. The first time you kissed. Winning the race. Nostalgia is laughter. Vacationing in your utopia. Exercising in a state of euphoria. It is found in the corner of your smile or the twinkle of your eye. It is hanging on wholeheartedly to the hint of remembered hope. The limitlessness of memories and infinite possibilities of hopes and dreams that you yearn to unlock. I don't only get nostalgic about my past and its colorful memories, I also get nostalgic over my future --- the unrehearsed, unseen of what's to come. At times, past life seems easier than trekking forward to an abyss of the unknown. On the other hand, dreaming of reaching the glistening light at the end of a stark tunnel can equally be nostalgic. Yeah, nostalgia is definitely a tingle. A tingle you've felt or long to feel.

Gone Lil' Black Girl

Gone lil' black girl
Two pigtails and one bang curl.
Snap your fingers
Lil' miss thing,
Rock your gumball jewelry
on that pinky ring.
Perfecting the eye roll,
Learn to stroll.
Walk with that switch,
that's in them hips,
Snap your neck
Suck your teeth like this.
Hula hoop girl,
Learn how your body swirls.
Double Dutch queen,
Peep the natural rhythm in me.
Playing jumping rope
Gold name tags 'round your throat
Door knockers in your ears,

Got that attitude to check those jeers.

Jelly shoes type of girl,

Living in Barbie's type of world.

Get your perm once a month,

Saturday cartoons

Eatin' Cap'n Crunch.

Momma's corn rowing your hair,

Get that kitchen, way back there.

Beads on ends, all different colors,

Grandma says you remind her of mother.

Gone lil' black girl,

In your black lil' world.

Learning your hand-clapping, knee-slapping sliding games,

Calling boys by silly names.

Sipping on the juice box,

Sucking on them lollipops.

Posted up on walls at malls,

Crushes of Immature lining bedroom walls,

Boys and Girls Club with your crew,

Chocolate baby

Do what you do.

Kenya dolls in all different colors,

Practice your own braiding technique

on the hair of your mother.

Playing with gymp

Boxes and barrels design

Life didn't matter,

My Chinese rope made Jacob's ladder.

My little pony

Kid Sister and me,

Bejeweled and bedazzled

Were my stonewashed jeans.

The beginning stages

of soft rhymes and vocals,

Expressing yourself

Stand out amongst the locals.

Summer time, kissed by the sun,

Gone lil' black girl

having fun.

Rollin' with her squad

Skate parties and such,

Slumber parties, laughing about much.

Scrunchies, fans and gel

to slap swirls in my hair,

didn't keep up with time

the day was labeled in my underwear.

Outside on the stoop

Playing with my Skip-It,

Tag, you're it

Oh, how I miss it!

Mother May I

Miss Mary Mack

go back to the days

of Patty Pat.

Where Cinderella,

Was Dressed in Yella',

Going upstairs

to kiss some fella.

Sitting on the rocker,

Eating Betty Crocker.

While folding up notes in class,

Playing M.A.S.H.

My prince was from

Bel-Air, -- where

Family always mattered,

Got in trouble in school

for having too much chit chatter.

Doing the cabbage patch

and the snake,

Beat boxing with the boys

Makin' brownies in my Easy Bake.

Gone lil' black girl

to them days long ago

Girl, you've aged,

those times were dope

These days I'm on a quest to find
My Chinese jump rope.

Ode to Vintage Summer

An Ode

Chlorine from public pools turns milk chocolate to a
deepened hue skin tone,
longer days prevent street lights from too quickly
escorting me home.
Days on the west side of town, double-dutched down
at the Boys & Girls Club,
Volunteering for free as a candy striper, working at
the movies for my first pay stub,
Early mornings and late afternoons of aiding momma
with the flowers and shrubs,
Late night sitting on the step in the 'burbs, watching
the mating game of lightning bugs.
Bicycling down Basin Road to the Battery Park with
dad,
'Til this day, I'm still a sucker for an afternoon with
some Smirnoff, some Ol' Bay and crabs.
Drugged up on antihistamines, pollen got the best of
me,

Think that was the first time I ever got stung by a honey
bee.
From plaits secured by colorful beads,
to micro-braids that I twirl 'round my fingers while
enjoyin' summer reads
that grab my attention and spark my curiosity
of the possibility of experiencing summer in the
Tanzanian Serengeti.
Family got together for holiday and 'just 'cuz'
barbecues,
the ability to rid socks and cop sandals and Old Navy
flip-flops – I was loving summer's shoes.
Annual trips to Virginia to visit Busch Gardens and Kings
Dominion,
summer nights are the greatest parts of life in my
humble opinion.
It's something 'bout bumpin' bass in the ride while
ripping' down I-95;
with the air off and windows down, and the elements of
the wind whipping my hair 'round.
The sound of music, attending festivals with steel
drums, the center of my core felt alive.
Summertime is like the West Coast way of life, it dilutes
all stress and strife
so relaxed, laid-back and never demanding,

the weather draws me to bodies of water, beaches and docks -- Penns Landing.

In need of a social life, must trek to the mall, at my mom, I fussed,

the first experience my childhood bestie and I had attempting to ride the city bus.

It holds the memory of when I first came into womanhood,

I, Hurston's Janie, attempting to get a grip of a developing woman misunderstood.

Life's fireworks - 4th of July's fireworks - an explosion of life for all to see,

Not for sure if I had summer or if summer was always having me.

Late night, cruising up the Pike to Philly with my squad in tow

Ready to Lambada, induced by lounges, liquor and lads,

If the walls of nightlife could talk, it might echo whispers of good girls gone bad,

If I could send a postcard to Summer, I'd sign it, " P.S. You're the best thing I ever had."

Now, each time I get in my whip and summer nights fall upon us,

Each time I turn on the station and Will Smith's spitting
that classic in mid-rhyme,
It's an instant reminder of the ebb and flow of my life
through
summer
summer
summer
time ... oooh, summertime.

Nerd-Girl Revenge

The following message is dedicated to my fellow
smart chicks.

The always-have-a-special-place-in-my-heart chicks.

You know the one.

Back in school, dudes wasn't fooling with.

Spent her days in Honors classes,

She stayed with hall passes,

She was the math whiz,

Who had all the answers

Hated PE ... no gymnastics,

And don't start tripping

She didn't sport glasses,

Or rock pocket protectors

She was semi-tight with the masses,

But only from the outskirts

Never quite passed it –

As the

super cool

super fly,

Cheerleading,

dating popular-quarterback-type of guy,

But I,

Would be a lie,

If I,

didn't recognize,

that I've,

more recently

caught his eye,

To his surprise,

Nice to meet ya

I'm "Jock"

Well I ...

I'm Tee,

You don't remember me?

From way back

With the flared jeans,

And the Reebok class – ic

No heels

No weaves,

Rocked buns and long sleeves.

I fooled

With that other crew,

You know who I'm referring to?

NOSTALGIA

The band geeks and drama freaks,

And she spent her weekends working,

And her weekdays studying,

Cuz she had aspirations,

Of walking

With college degree in hand,

Cuz in her family, that equated to the promise land,

And they don't understand

That no one had crossed it before

She studying so her momma,

One day, won't have to work no more.

And although dudes, she adored,

She had no time for

'Less it involved study sessions,

about academic progression --

And, she kept 'em guessing

She was extra chubby

Before big girls and thick girls were in -

And she was extra bubbly

Before nice attitudes and being genuine

was in -

So, being smart was her revenge,

And

She got straight A's on her

Report cards
To prove it
Intelligence, she used it!

Now, all of a sudden, she done became so fly
Cuz a fresh perm, good hair and a sharp eye --
Brow waxing
Got dudes tripping
Folks is looking
Swagger-jacking
Wardrobe tight from the
Crutch of her Essence and Cosmopolitan
she reads each night.

Looks can be so deceiving

So easy to change the outer

appearance

But the inside takes some seasoning

Inside, she's still that smart chick
That I got all this heart chick
That I don't fall for petty games
Hit the bull's-eye with my dart chick

NOSTALGIA

Slick tongue and quick wit

This is revenge, for my smart chicks

So take your TI-83s and your test tubes from Chemistry

And repeat this after me

I do solemnly swear

To never care

What other folks think of me.

So baby girl,

hold tight on to your book

and read on

about this big ol' world.

Leave the later on

to be carrying on

But being "that" girl.

And honestly,

I'd rather have real rap

About Socrates and philosophies

and Shakespeare and Paul Revere

and the irony of logic and math,

you can find it here.

For years,

I've always been more attracted by the mental

And what you can do with that pencil

And what theologies and ideologies you in to

More than how you can handle

That ball or this bat
Or how you slick talk
Your way back
In and out of drama
I'm the one you want to
Bring home to your momma
And I realized,
That once those 20's hit
And school is out of session,
It's that smart chick
Providing you life lessons.
Yet, you still second guessing ...

Vacationing In

Write
Light --- the candles,
that surround me.
Pen and pad in hand.
I demand -
this.
The hues of browns
and oranges astounding --
Me.
Water that trickles
down the rocks from underneath.
Serenity and peace.
Black art of various shades
Parade
the loft's walls.
Essence magazines
lay at my feet.
Books by Souljah, Tyree, poetry,
my floetry – complete.

The scents of vanillas
And mangos soothe
My nostrils.
Silence- except my simple breath
It echoes
Bouncing 'round rooms.
The feeling consumes -- me.
I breathe.
Chai tea-
brown sugar and cream.
The subtle sound of
Water flowing downstream.
Large, fluffy pillows
Concave to my frame.
The softness of the beige
couch do the same.
Music spinning the passion
of neo-soul and jazz.
Warm knitted blanket
acts as --
another layer of skin.
Today, I'm vacationing in.
The taste of seafood and sushi
Dance on my tongue.

No work to be done.

Sparkle glistens from the

Glass of white wine.

No sense of time.

I unwind.

Was a Good Day

Today was a good day.
A, I'm so glad the sun decided to shine bright, day
A, thankful for the air that keeps me cool at night,
day
A, my health is cool, my teeth are white, day
A, I've got a mind, a hand and a pen to write, day
A, the bills are paid, even if my pockets are light, day
A, Bob Marley, everything is going to be alright, day
A, J.J. from Good Times 'cuz I'm dynamite, day
A, I've got shoes and clothes, even if they fitting
tight, day
A, I've got a clan of family and friends, even if we
fight, day
A, I have a career and car to get me up that Pike,
day
A, I took the time to volunteer for someone else's
plight, day
A, I've persevered and succeeded amid all faces

white, day

A, I got a good dose of morals and knowing wrong from
right, day

A, my mind sparked his interest, so he wanted to grab a
bite, day

A, they were living in the dark, and I got to shed some
light, day

All in all ...

Even when skies are gray,

My mind is what decided to call today an alright day

Life and death are in the power of the tongue,

So I speak light in appreciation of
the Son.

I Had a Dream

I had a dream.

Something the size of Martin Luther King,

But, instead of letting it ring

On mountain tops and valley lows,

Or the alleys of inner city ghettos,

In the internal caves of my mind,

It echoes

And tugs on my heart

Each time the wind blows;

Or the beat drops,

Imagine Picasso painting masterpieces

On top -

A brownstone's rooftop,

Or Beethoven playing a symphony

On a rugged piano held up by cinderblocks;

See, that's artistry

At its very best,

Making something out of nothing

Creativity, yes!

Finding the rose in the cement,

Appreciating the gray-scale in a silhouette;

Or possibly -

Waves crashing,

Sun rising;

Moon tides,

Sweet lullabies,

I excavate the beauty

I am inspired by life -

Or music ... my muse

Or dance ... its moves,

All things creative ... I use

As a weapon,

Motivating me to write.

I had a dream

that I feared would get deferred,

so I wrote my existence

and birthed such reality

Question is: Does yours go unheard?

Dreams of Being a Soulful Chick

A French Kyrielle

I wanted to cut my perm out
Grow dreads the length of the Nile's mouth
My momma did not like that pitch
Dreams of being a soulful chick.

So, I did pierce my nose instead
and penned the thoughts that swarmed my head
I love the arts and politics
Dreams of being a soulful chick.

If I could have the job I dream,
I'd be with Essence magazine
I'd sip on tea; watch urban flicks
Dreams of being a soulful chick.

I'd wear a black fist on my shirt

NOSTALGIA

No shoes so I could feel the Earth
Bangles on wrist, you'd hear them click
Dreams of being a soulful chick.

Buy product from black vendor store
My "sista," I'd never ignore
I am so Afrocentric
Dreams of being a soulful chick.

I'd paint and dance, express myself
Use change, not bills- enhance my wealth
Giving of self, it makes me rich
Dreams of being a soulful chick.

I'd be conscious and read a lot
I'd talk about "systems" and "plots"
I'd rock the mic and talk liiiike thhiiissss
Dreams of being a soulful chick.

Full of expression would be me
My thoughts run deep as the blue sea
I would be really passionate
Dreams of being a soulful chick.

Au naturel and burn incense

And speak out on unjust nonsense
I'd have self-love; a free spirit
Dreams of being a soulful chick.

I never lived inside the box

One day, I will have my dreadlocks
Live in brownstone made out of bricks
Dreams of being a soulful chick.

Music

A Double Acrostic

Moves me to the rhythms of my favorite ja**m**

Undulating my hips effortlessly to a beat blaring

from the wetlands of a bayo**u**

Soothes the tears of my spirit from inflicting

debris while sitting in the church pew**s**

Inspires me to achieve by commissioning my

destiny's alib**i**

Conjuring up elated memories all the while

grooving in my mind to its acousti**c**

Mystical Music

You are the only person that I always listen to
Since my conception, I've watched as culture
changes you
Or maybe it is you that changes it
You've got your own melodic language
I'm in love with your tempo and versatility,
Whether jazz, neo-soul, gospel, hip-hop or R&B
My appreciation for you is the greatest when I'm
alone
Only you know how to get me into the zone
My self-appointed psychiatrist
Never need I say much, you always get the gist
Your tunes speak to my array of moods, emotions
and situations
I will always keep your essence in heavy rotation
Never thought that my first Jodeci cassette would
turn into this,
Listening to you can craft a tear, draw anger or birth

bliss

A full-fledge obsession

Music, you're always teaching me a lesson

Each time I see you, it's a trip down memory lane

While I'm grateful for all senses, I'd give up my sight for you to remain.

If Poetry didn't mind, I'd have a second affair with you.

An instrumental tunnel, you're always putting me through -

No other art form imaginable can speak to me like you do.

I sing and hum, you're always on my mind

A consistent staple in life, you will always evolve with time

you move mental mountains and heal heartfelt heartache

Speak trans all language while erupting emotional earthquakes.

You've always accepted me for who I am

More than a listen, a head bob or a dance;

you own the jam

you set my mind euphorically into trances

by embodying my expression in audible romances.

The sound you serenade swallows me quick with one

switch

A melting pot you created: rhythm, timbre, texture and
pitch

Just the taste of you sends me into a fit

Your rhythms pour passion down my ears

You unintentionally unmask my fears

Music: The one thing I've listened to over the years.

New York

I lived you.

Danced in the artery of your heart.

Crooned like crimson amid the ancestral pathway of
the renaissance.

I heard your heartbeat

It exhilarated me.

Made my hips sway and rhythm move.

I floated on your stage.

Wrapped myself in its curtains.

A chorus line of you.

They recognized me, like long-lost relatives.

Welcomed me home as if I had never left.

I lived you.

Took a boy in awe of your being.

Beautifully, rigidly, ruggedly crafted.

Puzzle fit perfect to me

Towers towering like trees above me.

The people, its branches.

I wanted to bury myself in your boroughs.

Get lost in the love of you.

I paid homage to you.

I lived you.

You fed me enriched nectar of your soul.

It soothed my core.

Your culture nourishes my malnourished mind.

You teach me people

You make me sing the caged bird's creed.

I caught you in the pit of my stomach

Tears of joy and feelings unknown make-up'd my face

I lived you.

Rode and explored your ebb and flows.

Witnessed the poverty of stories untold.

You breed unsung heroes.

You grant and shatter dreams.

The epitome of life's reality.

You are my spirit's mother.

I never knew I belonged to you.

I lived you.

The lights drew me near, and I came home.

Never felt so alive.

It was you all along.

You are the hook and beat of my song.

The world was still and life made sense.

NOSTALGIA

You were calling me.
You've been calling me.
I picked up the phone and came home.
I lived you.

Nostalgia

I heard sight

I watched smell

I inhaled taste

I savored touch

I felt sound

and the in-betweens were senseless.

Chapter 4

DEGREES OF LOVE

This chapter is possibly the most near and dear to my heart and soul. It is me. It is my experiences with love. After all, I'm a woman. We love, and we love hard. Sometimes, we love blindly. Other times, we love consciously. Yet, we were built to love passionately. I love colorfully through a variety of seasons. I love at various degrees and temperaments. It is my desire that you are able to let down your full guard and allow your heart to become intertwined amid the lines you are about to read. I'm certain you will relate to some poems, learn from some poems and most importantly, appreciate the true essence of love at its core. Regardless of my experiences with love … some beautiful, others painful, I would be remiss if I were to say I didn't value the lessons learned during the ebbs and flows and in-betweens of life through love. Do remember this: It is impossible to love another selflessly without loving yourself first selfishly.

Game of Life

He and I would connect four hours
Amid my attempt at a trivial pursuit of life,
With a strong desire, he'd rack my cranium
Because I played it just right.
He told me I was a slice of perfection,
And in me, he had found a healthy obsession
With me he wanted to take his time,
For I turned him on, and I'd boggle his mind.
And if I could drive love's wheel of fortune,
He'd hope I wouldn't drive towards him blind.
I told him this wouldn't be an easy operation
'Cuz matters of the heart, to me, were taboo
That he'd regret this, be sorry if only he knew
I was trouble; he wouldn't catch my charade or clue
I even warned him if I had to identify a soul mate
I'd be unable to truly guess who?
He promised me he'd rid all chutes and ladders
That would come in the way of what he'd build for us,

That life would be a sweet trip down candy land,
If I'd honor his hand and give him my trust.
He challenged me to just break the ice,
Let down my guard, and treat him right
For I could face the truth, or dare a lie,
I submitted -- I'd become quite fond of this fine guy.
He'd ostracized my heart, become its monopoly
Even as I struggled to put my peace at jeopardy,
He reassured me if I just take this risk
With him, the game of life would be a whisk.

Cereal Courtship

He 'Tony the Tiger'-ed her
Got her feeling all grreeeeaaaaattttt!
She even eating her Wheaties now
Got shawty sipping on a bottle of V8
Silly girl, she never learned that Trix's were for kids
Got her going coo coo for Cocoa Puffs
Even though their Cheerios were short lived.
And while there's more in Life to debate,
That's neither here nor there
Because now, her punctuation mark is late
From being reckless with her Frosted Flakes
Back against the wall, fresh out of Lucky's Charm
There's no pot of gold at the rainbow's end
Just some senseless lil' Leprechaun
So now she's left Raisin' his Bran
Life changes got her Fruit Looped
Meanwhile, Mr. Tony the Tiger
Well, like Toucan Sam, he flew the coop.

Left Honey Combs alone with this Kix at her side.
This new little Mini Wheat will become the Apple Jacks
of her eye.
She prays he'll grow up to be a Special K or a Krispie's
Treat.
All this because his daddy didn't want her Total package
And just wanted some Cinnamon Buns to beat.
After Captain Crunch had his Banana Nut
He left her empty without a Fruity Pebble
Because his Grape Nuts were on some other type of
level.
Next time, she'll learn to keep them Honey Smacks in
Chex
Leave the Quaker Oats for the next
So when Toni ask what he's eating for breakfast,
She can say Nut n' Honey, 'cuz for him, there will be
nothing left.

Anew

Hey baby
How could you
Could you
Could we
Start over again
Anew.
There's something
Special
Refreshing
That me have always
seen in you.
There's a glitch
Switch
Flicker in your eye.
I won't lie
I
Can be difficult at times.
Time is of the essence

Essentially
I just want to
Unwind us again.
Could we switch?
About face
Rewind
The hands of time.
Hey baby
Could you
Could we
Start forever
Again?

Chocolate Rain

Essence drips

from the tips

of your spirit's lips

like chocolate syrup mixed --- with honey.

Honey, you melt me sweet.

I just want to take a swim or dip downstream, diving

in the direction of your mind.

'Cuz it boggles me into frenzy.

Leaving me enigma'd as to how you could be.

So perfectly crafted and packaged effortlessly

from inner to exterior.

At times, I can't help but stare at that ---

Manifestation that formulated you.

It perfectly staing my views.

And you?

You are a trip. Literally. I fall.

As I watch you slip from underneath of me

the pages from amid my heart's history,

and recreate the storyline of my favorite movie.

Unbeknownst to you, you turn me.

Spin me --- in ways I thought I could never pirouette.

Your words often cause my mind to arabesque.

I point my toes at the thought of you.

I adore thee -- time we spend together.

You presence is luring.

I'm often left a fish, exploring -- you in arrays of weather.

And whether, sunshine or rain,

Long walks or leaned against car window panes,

I'd walk a million miles to be mentally awakened by your brain.

Yeah, it's that deep.

Not enough nights to sleep

Away the effects of you.

Generosity and compassion exude from you.

I am wooed by you.

Moved by you.

Moved by your attention to my detail

Like you're trying to interpret the blueprint of my grayscale

I can tell --- that you dig the small stuff I'm into.

It's in the thickness of the air we share.

I swear, infrequently, I catch and feel the ending of your

stare.

Captivating.

Stimulating.

Breath. Breathe. Thief! 'cuz my air you're taking.

A fiend, I'm often left awaiting --- my next fix of you.

Mental masturbation --- my mind replaying time with you.

In wonderment and the anticipation

Of the next time you'll rain on me --

real chocolately-like.

A Rise and Fall

I took a ride that rose and fell
In sync with the rise and fall of my breast atop your
chest.
We were the only participants.
All the while were estranged immigrants to each
other;
Desired lovers in a foreign exchange of a deranged
road where plutonic friends meet pleasure
The forbidden fruit that is often mentally devoured
and never physically digested,
I'd never guessed it – fate – would place us here,
In your place, with pressed bodies, and let's face it,
the ere of ecstasy near
Isn't no denying it, won't lie to it,
Put a Bible, an oath and alibi to it!
If you were a stranger, I would have engaged a kiss
As if they held the muscle of the tongue that exists
between your lips.
As fully-clothed, we rode a ride to the rise and fall of

your breath
That massaged life's stress away while I lie tightly atop
your chest.
But, this isn't as easy as life would have it,
A mutually non-exclusive amicable friendship has
already been established.
That prevented our ability to drench in chocolate and
dip,
But trip at the sight of passion that poured from the
parting of my lips,
I'm certain you're fully aware
Is that why you refuse to lock too long in a tango of
glance and stare?
The tension was there
I'd tear a trail of it, in order to break the burden to bear
—
If I, had I, would I ... we wouldn't, we couldn't, we
shouldn't
So, I ride this out as a passenger, lie atop the moment
as a friend
Realizing the danger that awaits if we pretend
For a moment that we were strangers
That there was no tomorrow
That a heated moment wouldn't end in sorrow

That there weren't expectations to live up to

No realities to wake up to

No hearts to protect from breaking

But in this moment, your chest was my safe haven,

It was the embracing my mental ignored while my body
was craving.

While my breast lie atop your chest ----

I could hear Heaven whisper in my eardrum

And soothe my spirit sounding like the womb of a conch
shell

All while our breast and chest simultaneously rose and
fell.

Homecoming

I squint my eyes inquisitively at the sight of your
silhouette.
Sensing a distant resemblance, but I'm uncertain
how we initially met.
It's disheartening to my spirit how soon we both
forget.
But I know you.
I am certain I do.
There was a time that I was very close to you.
I believe there's a rib that I owe to you.
It's ironic that what we go through --
Forgets to bring us back to where we came from.
You were the King, and I was the Queen of a sacred
kingdom.
You were the answer to my spirit's religion.
I've been desperately waiting
In anticipation of your lead to take us on a Middle
Passage Mecca home.
My soul has been trying

Dying

Crying for you to reclaim your throne.

I believe we've lost sight of what we were purposely
designed to do.

Centuries have passed since I've last spoken to you.

The summer of 1618 whispers the last time I made love
to you.

Don't you hear the tears of my soul calling you,
Hannibal?

I answer them as Nefertiti.

As a memoir to our love, I will tattoo the graffiti of it across the auras of the African sky ---

It is my lasting attempt to return home to the Bush as
your budding bride.

Consider it a pseudo S.O.S. to scribe an alibi that the
union of us was never a lie.

It isn't a figment of their historical imagination.

I was your wife.

You were my life.

So, believe me when I scribe that ---I know you.

I was close to you.

I'm certain our vows are buried somewhere beneath a

sweeping sand in the Serengeti.

It was the reception place to where we were married.

If only we could go back ... get back ... to that sacred space

For what we've evolved into has caused our ancestral dynasty a disgrace.

We were Africa, and it was divine.

That was before your hands were forcefully pulled from the intertwining of mine.

I remember the time.

My King, I yearn to feel home. Are you ready to take me there?

It is guaranteed you'd recognize me if you'd just take the time to stop and stare

For you, I will haste --- pack my things, ready and prepare

I know what it must be like raisin a sun off the strange fruit of their lies

Don't you see the topography of the Motherland tracing the corners of my eyes?

It will take all that is left in us to right this wrong.

Do you hear the vibrations of the Djembe drum playing our wedding song?

I know you do.

Because I know you.
You are my King.
And I promise you —
When you summon for me.
I will remember you
And we will go home.

Enigma

Stream of Consciousness

I pictured you as a sweet hobby
that I'd dabble with from time to time.
You were a melted snowflake
on the tip of a muted tongue.
A soldier's Purple Heart.
The last breath of life.
You are fang.
My refugee.
A painted mural canvassing a ghetto ruin.
You are symphony
Depicted beautifully.
I call you masterpiece.
Crafted so magnificently.
Air.
The finishing line.
The sun rays glistening on tranquil water.
You taste like peace.

Walk like confidence.
Feel like utopia.

I find you midway past the book's cover.

Sleeping peacefully in a corner.

Suspended in air.

You are lavender.

Love and passion.

A dressed up smile.

A piercing stare.

You tissue dry my tears.

Peel open a cold heart.

You are a touchdown.

A dream undeterred.

A roaring laughter that rolls rhythmically.

Love.

Love.

Love.

There is subtle simplicity about you.

A drumbeat --- more specifically, its high hat.

A violin.

Trumpet ... wait, no, saxophone.

Yes, bass saxophone.

You are a BASS saxophone.

Electricity runs through your veins.

I see the reflection of God in you.

Feel His heartbeat through you.

An aura sky.

Sweet lullaby.

Butterflies.

A lion.

A roaring royal lion.

You ooze wisdom and complexity.

You are my missing link.

My spirit's Adam.

He Showers Me

He flowers me --- pardon, I mean showers me
With rose petals
That must have been grown in soil descending from
the Heavens.

He is heaven to me.

Our exchanges simile so heavenly.
I'll be his angel.
Yes, I'll be his angel that guards his heart.
For life eclipses in the mere seconds that we're
apart.
He is a work of art.
I strive to be Mona Lisa –
Unleashing the –
Infinite powers I internally possess –
In an attempt to devour his happiness;
In exchange for an eternity in euphoria.
My love, I want to explore the –
Numerous, infinite possibilities that love adds to us.
All the while he just –

Wants to flower me, pardon, I mean shower me

With petals upon petals of his love

That stem –

From roots planted deep within

The intricate crevasses of his heart.

And his blood? --

Like nectar that nourishes and fertilizes our growth.

That is why I love him the most.

He sees to it that we never depart

By pollinating, yes, feverishly –

Pouring the scent of his essence into me.

But, in the times when we must,

He sends waves of himself by way of cupid's harp.

Pulling on its strings to make the sound of us vibrato –

'Til the world knows he is summoning me.

I am his message in a bottle.

We are love, full throttle

I want to swallow … my pride

And submit for the opportunity to walk by his side

To become his bride.

I-

Oh my

I-

Why --

He takes me there.

And I just stare
Yes, look
And stare
At this creature that has been placed
On this Earth for me.
He is the key –
To my enigma
Answers my soul's puzzles effortlessly.
How could this be?
When he just
See, he just
Yes, he --
Just wants to flower me – pardon,
I mean shower me with his love.

Soul Full

If you only knew
What it is you do.
It exists in the influx of your tone when you address
me.
In the warmth of the air when you're next to me.
You equate to ecstasy.
You bring out the best in me.
You crazily amaze me incredibly.
You have the tendency to fuel the chemistry that
zealously remedies my inferiorities.
You guaranty the destiny of our moment's melody, so
heavenly.
My soul has been engaged to you
Before a breath of opportunity to engage with you
By pure destiny, I'd moment an exchange with you
That intertwined a tango of consonant and vowels
My whole, I vow to be yours.
Bow, in an opportunity to explore

All that God has willed us have in store.

Yesterday seems like forever whenever it's the last time
we've been together.

I'd cleverly weather the storm for you.

And drench a cloud full of love for you

That pours hotter than sunny rays on a blizzard day.

You Can't Contain Love

You can't contain love.

Can't shove love in the corner of your hallway closet in hopes of no one uncovering it.

You can't contain it.

Can't rid it beneath a trashcan lid, and send it out for where the county dump lives.

Nope, you sure as hell can't contain love.

Can't tuck love neatly underneath your pillow to visit it only in your dreams.

Can't bury it beneath a rapid stream of an obscure reality.

Can't tie it bound to the ground, for it is sure to be found ---

Lying about, 'round the remnants of where its sunshine awakens your spirit.

For it will drip off the tip of your pen.

Linger in the crease of your smile.

Flicker in the speck of your eye.

Show a side of you most hadn't seen in a while.

I hear it in resonating in the ending of your laughter.

Felt it in the hug that came thereafter.

Smell it subtly intertwined in your scent.

So, unto the Heavens, I'll proclaim and vent

You can't contain love.

Can't ssshhh it neither.

Can't tell it to be mindful of all those who stop, stare

and glare ---

At the audacity of you being happy, either.

You damn sure can't contain love.

Love won't even let you walk the same.

Baby, you don't even talk the same.

So who you think you fooling with this I'm-not-in-love

game?

For in the midst of your attempts to contain,

Love will grow like a rose amid concrete

Will rise, without discrete, like a Phoenix from the valley

peaks of hate's ashes

and seek to transform metaphysically mid-air into a

willed dove that soars, bearing

the weight of your love.

'Cuz real love ...

Real love ---- you can't contain.

Fireworks

Your spirit is like milk chocolate dipped in complexity
and sprinkled with perfection.
I got a mental erection every time we speak.
And when we meet?
Fireworks!
Literally
You shed a certain light on me.
Rekindle this flame inside me.
That hasn't flickered or been turned on in years.
Amid the naysayers and jeers,
I am comforted by your cheers.
You're not so subtle exclamations of admirations of
who I am.
The woman I have become.
You are my number one -- man.
And I, your fan.
Life with you is a whirlwind of happiness.
I am my happiest each time we speak.

And when we meet?

Fireworks!

Both literally and figuratively.

Fireworks!

Bursting at my seams and oozing out of my pores

Fireworks!

It is you that I admire and adore.

Fireworks!

That consumes me from heart, head to toe

Fireworks!

Exuding from my essence this effervescent, iridescent glow

Fireworks!

Breath-taking, earth shaking, love-making

Fireworks!

I pant, heat racing for what's in store

Fireworks!

Each combustion has me yearning for more

Fireworks!

Of you ...

Cocoa-Brown Angels

I want to make cocoa-brown chocolate covered
angels
That adorn halos freshly dipped in caramel,
Wings made of butterscotch
That grace my jaw line with Hershey kisses.
I want to make cocoa-brown chocolate covered
angels
That bear the sweet message of God.
Almond-shaped eyes made of amber
With a mane made of jet bronze silk.
Teeth like chocolate diamonds.

They will speak honey.
Will interpret the Psalms in amaretto.
Cry in a Negro falsetto.

With an undertone of cinnamon.
I want to make cocoa-brown chocolate covered
angels

With blood the shade of ink

That smell like fresh brewed coffee mixed with toffee

A deportment sacredly crafted of terracotta

Topped off with lips that kiss sepia

I want to make cocoa-brown chocolate covered angels

With spines of iron

A mental the depth of midnight

Skin as thick as oil

A soul deeply rooted in an Obsidian soil

Tanned hands that harvest life

Words as rooted as ginger

I want to make cocoa-brown chocolate covered angels

with you

Underneath a mahogany tree

With your mocha syrup wrapping me

tightly --- like linen

Careful not to imperfect your seed

that will birth our melanin legacy.

Yin and Yang Love

I muse him.

I approve of him.

He is my King.

For him, I will sing his praise.

Of him, I am in complete amazement.

He amazes me.

I will be his Queen.

I Rosie the Rivet his spirit.

Make ripples in his bath water.

He Malcolm X's me by any means.

I shape apples in his eyes.

He is my Lion.

I, a black pearl.

I'm THAT girl to him.

Better yet, his woman.

Best yet, his wife.

He ribbed me life.

I am forever indebted to him.

We are priceless.

He is yin.

We are chocolate syrup, and I ooze caramel for his
honey.

Strong is he.

I belong to he.

He is onyx to me.

Our love composes music – orchestrated symphonies.

We recreate history --

And willed us to belong together.

We transcend time forever.

I evolve around his moon.

I am his shining star.

He propels my spirit afar.

We gazelle through life.

I am the day, and he is my night.

I am a volcano and he, the calm sea.

Strangely, he has the ability to calm me.

Soothing is his aura.

His voice trumpets my mind.

A falsetto.

I've grown fond of him with time.

He is it for me.

There was no before and will be no after.

This is it for me.

He conjures fear, cheers, love and laughter.

He has sought after --- my heart and won.

I am done.

He has captured me in his embrace.

He is the better half of our one.

I am his grace.

He covers my Achilles and I, his backside

A modern day Bonnie and Clyde.

I am yang.

I am lung, and he is my air.

We lock stares.

Entering me commences his Mecca home.

We zone.

It is us against this world alone.

He is my Yin

And I am his Yang,

And we are love.

It Is Love

It is found in the dry ground,
seconds before the first rain of a season.
It is the smell of fried fish battered in
cornmeal and paprika against olive oil.
It hovers above the valleys of nature,
before the sunrise or down of the day.
It is heard in the midst of night between the
crickets shrill and hoot of the owl.
It nestles itself in the entanglement of one's bowels.
It is felt like the beat of an African Djembe drum
in the hot desert of Sahara.
It tastes sweeter than fresh honey dripping
from the womb of a bee.
It is more illuminating to visualize than the Auroras
that
ascend upon the nocturnal skies of the Poles.
It is deeper than diving into an abyss that's bottom
resembles the mantle of Earth's core.
It is heard in the vibrato belted out from the mouth

of the saxophone's soothing sound.

It is seen in the adjoining of sand shores and current
waves
crashing against the ocean.

It is moister than imparting lips mixed with ineffable,
tender tears.

It is tracing along the follicle timeline of grayed-haired
couples to their jovial roots.

It is more vivid than the residue of the rainbow
covenant seen after the storm.

It is the merging of a couplet, to a mono-being that
forms.

It is felt in the spiritual embrace of intertwined souls.

It is the changing of the seasons from seed, stem to full
bloom.

It is more miraculous than opaque craters that align the
moon.

It is more complete than the 360 degree of a circle and
axis.

It is intense.

It is the smell of burnt wool from a sacrificial
lamb on Abraham's altar in lieu of his son.

It is more breathtaking than the composition of the
Seychelles Islands that decorate the Indian Ocean.

It is devotion.

It is the time that exists between the present and the
motionless hand of an antique Victorian grandfather
clock.

It is the thick air that exists amongst strangers
when their pupils lock.

It is more potent than the elixir shared between the
heirs of the Capulet's and Montague's.

It skews.

It is patient and kind.

Purer than a white dove.

It is agape.

It is love.

Fading Indigo
A Diamante

Purple

Power, Royal

Intriguing, Appealing, Empowering

Wisdom, Imperial, Ignorance, Peasant

Depressing, Uninspiring, Boring

Dull, Common

Gray

Disillusioned

My thoughts of you
Have drifted from somewhere between certainty
to a bit confused.
Slightly disillusioned.
Might be my fault,
to quick to abuse my heart ---
Then label it love and wear it on my sleeves.
Hopeless romantic mixed with a bit of free
spiritedness
is the Sagittarius' pet peeve.
Often times, I'm at loss for what I attempt to
achieve.

I am no different.
For instance,
I've played this role before.
Read this script.
I even wrote it.

Been praying that my spirit burned the manuscript.

Thought I'd eventually, habitually, forget it.

This feeling.

Love.

'Cuz I often obscure it somewhere between

lust and infatuation --- sprinkled with a little boredom.

Come ... no go ... wait, I'm not done.

My entertainment, tap dance for me.

Tap a little harder - LOUDER.

Seconds later, wonder how the heck

did you get here, and who let you in?

Me

I am the one with the key.

I am the one who left the gate open.

Now you're waiting, hoping --

Truly, I'm the one to blame.

Loving and lusting and voids that still remain.

Somewhere defragmented in me.

I envy warmed hearts of my peers

Mine been chilled on ice for years.

Distant Love

He sits less than five feet away,
But his love feels so distant.
Within an instant,
It fades from shades of reds
To hues of gray.
And I pray
That my love
Would be enough
To revitalize his senses
And end this
Senseless form of compassion,
For I fashion
A different side of him.
That reveals the real passionate side in him.
On the contrary, he sits less than five feet away
But feels more than a hundred miles at bay,
Growing even more distant with time and each day.
In many different ways
Though, I'm speechless

147

Lord, I ask, and I pray
Direct appropriate words to say
I love you --
And I'm here to stay
And if it be your will
May that red be restored from shades of gray.

Ten Minutes Or Less

Ten minutes or less
Is all the time I possess
To prove love to you.
Ten minutes or less
Not enough time to express
My unwavering love for you.
Ten minutes or less
The clock's ticking, still I confess
My inability to get by without you
There's no rainbow nor sky without you
Honey tastes bitter and dry without you
Oceans don't crash or tide without you
Gazelles don't propel nor glide without you.
My Cherie, there's no Amour without you
Three don't precede four without you
The valves of my heart don't endure without you
All blues and no rhythm without you
Heart beats are staccato without you
Yo no puedo pensado without you

Mi alma esta desesperado without you

LaBelle's note don't vibrato without you

Mi corazon doesn't give love without you

I'm on an ark without a fig and dove without you

There's no natural high without you

No answers or reasons or why's without you

The Mediterranean runs dry without you

No apple for my eye without you

Ten minutes or less

I'm trying my very best,

But the fact remains, I'm Juliet

And Romeo, true love means I'd die

without you.

Catastrophic Love

Seven hundred, eighty-nine dollars and ninety-five
cents
was how much it cost
to replace the window after you tossed
my vanity dresser across
my bedroom that night.
It's funny what you'd never confess aloud
that you feel at liberty to write.
And while time heals all wounds,
both I and my bedroom
are left with the scar,
Sailing rapidly from love afar
and a nightmare to share
from when you didn't care
and horded a hurricane in my bedroom that night.
The moment I realized your Jekyll and Hyde side
and Frankenstein-tattered heart.
Determined to love you
like no one else ever would or will

after a better understanding of your past,

I gathered why you'd routinely morph into steel.

But still,

I tried to peel

away at the onion

and reveal

your bud.

I would just think --- he just needs love.

So, love, I brought to you,

transported it on a shopping cart for you

from the frozen food aisle

to symbolize

its inability to rot or spoil.

You had me coiled

'round your finger.

In a weary web of preconceived notions of love and lie.

Your type of love needed an alibi.

It'd go missing for weeks on end

while my heart's veins were left to shrivel up and die.

Not sure if this situation is better or worse than

infidelity,

At least then I could have something tangible to blame.

But, instead of a being, you cheated on me with your

battered, bruised heart and brain.

That'd play tricks on you

that I was left to solve the enigmas of you.

'Cuz the moment life had lemonade you,

You forget that I was by your side.

The Bonnie to your Clyde

Your ride or die.

I -

I watched you metamorphose from man to beast

And single-handedly, emotion-evoked banded

flail my fifty-pound vanity

set and dresser drawers

across the room that night.

Thought my mind was playing tricks on my sight.

This has got to be some insecure trick's movie, right?

Right ...

A victim of self-pity, insecurity --- you were destined to

doom.

And I --- I to climb out of your abyss

And revisit

the flickering light in me that had always existed,

The one I didn't want to let shine 'round you.

Rather be miniscule so you could grow grandeur 'round

you.

'Til it became hard to pacify my life 'round you.

I was designed after Christ, he just hadn't found you.

Or you him ---

And while there were sunny days,

You never understood the definition of love's vibrant rays.

Misused and abused my internal prescription for love

To self-medicate you, love

To rehabilitate you, love

Yet never did you understand how to reciprocate my love.

An unexcavated treasure,

I wanted to measure

off a surmountable amount of agape

and auction it up to you for free.

No cost

No charge

Just a warranty and unconditional guarantee.

So, I was at lost for words

As I watched this man that I adored

Metamorphosed into a beast and flail effortlessly my dresser drawers.

Broken glass and shattered dreams.

Things aren't always as they seem.

So yes, that's what happens when a tornado meets a
volcano,
something is bound to rip at the seam.
And I'll admit, while I was doing what I was supposed
to,
we women have a way in provoking you,
and I lit the match that ignited that fire
that sparked that squabble
that night.
Tears and verbal venom spewed
While shoved bones and walls and doors
and all else that love could no longer endure
Poured
Leaked
And ran wretched and rapid 'round my bedroom walls
and carpeted floor.
And as the vanity mirror went flying,
destined to crash against the bedroom window,

our love went dying

and shattered pieces of it lie beneath the seal embran-
gled with hate's glass.
Alas ...no, let's admit it
Trained to persevere, I couldn't quit this
I still didn't leave.

Pride in the way, desire to help you self-medicate
and heal your grief.
But, I'm not your Savior nor am I some type of esteemed
police.
Repeated trips to the well,
and you still wouldn't drink.
I keep that twisted memory and Lowes window receipt,
and each time I crawl in my bed to sleep
And out my new bedroom window I peep,
I am reminded of what happens
When you love too deep
'Cuz the next time
Might have been my last time
If he replaced the drawer and window and instead, flung
me.
So, while I lost my vanity,
I gained my sanity
and the ability to write this candidly
You CAN put a price tag on love -
My life is priceless.
And it only cost him seven hundred and eighty-nine dol-
lars and ninety-five cents ... and me.

What's My Name

You never saw me.

Just saw what you wanted.

Franted -- On me.

So now you're confused.

Confused at how I could be,

This muse.

With the ability

to move a crowd.

You slept on the butterfly in me.

Rarely noticed the caterpillar.

You tell me I've changed.

I tell you

You never took the time.

Never took the time

to really get to know me.

Genuinely.

To uncover my layers.

And I wouldn't shed them for you.

For fear you wouldn't protect

The inner me.

Neglect the Queen in me.

So now you challenge me.

With an audacity to tell me

Quite drastically

I never let you in my world.

But I find it hard.

Hard to understand

Your desire to want

To be in my presence

When you —

Don't even beam

When I walk into yours.

You think you know me.

But you don't even know my name.

Never took the time to say it.

Spell it.

Practice writing it in cursive.

Or my favorite color

or food.

You can't even detect

a frequency change in my mood.

Because you never saw me.

Just saw what you wanted.

Fronted -- On me.

Proper Closure

It was all in the thickness of that pregnant pause,

Caught up in an awkward clause of silence and speak

I seek

To explain my past actions to you

Former lover, I know that I've hurt you

And while unable to undo this web of hurt

That we've both had a part in tying,

I'm here to explain while I went flying when love went dying.

Yes, we're over done.

No, I'm not the one --- for you.

I'm sorry if falling out of me hurt you.

I do.

So caught up in the thickness of that pregnant pause
Was the heartbeat of our flagrant flaws

That all but tarnished our love.

I'll always love you.

But the thought of being in, I've decided against.

Yes, I'm out.

I've thrown in the towel.

And it's funny how

when I look at the dried up remnants of our love

that lay as residue on it, I'm not left

tarnished or squandering the thought of harnessing it ---

Just caught up somewhere

between a clause and this pregnant pause

of silence

that beats so figuratively loud in perfect harmony

to the echoes of my ear's canals and my heart

As our two-step of perfect harmony

Drifts and dwindles apart and all that is left to do

is to conclude farewells and bid adieu

And marvel at the residue of our love

that lie shriveled gently atop the towel

we both threw in.

Pickettin' White Fences

From a slumber I wake
From a restless night I shake -
Off the thoughts of you
That cloud the psyche of my mind
And pray to God, in time
The remnants of us
Are left behind.
And my mind?
She plays tricks on me
She been told me that love was blind.
So I asked Helen Keller to show me
her view of the world,
'Cuz mine
Was obviously skewed by
this little girl.
Who had big dreams of a chocolate man
And this wicked plan -
Of marriage with white picket fences
and 2.4 kids and -

Living on some distant land.

So, tonight ---

I'm picketing white fences

and storybook princes

'Cuz my imageries of being Cinderella -

are senseless.

Forgetting to question if this generic future was -

We ... mine ... or his...

And did I ever mention

It was never my intention

To fall so deep into

A relationship with you.

'Cuz how things went so rapidly from summer nights

to me quickly referring to you as

My boo --

I never knew,

And before either of us knew

A full relationship had ensued.

Truth be told, I wish this story shorter

Therefore, I could draft a simple haiku.

But, so quickly

We women

Get so wrapped up

In these men

and fascinated by dating
We can't stand the thought
of waiting
We never ask the basics -- like
Is dude a Christian?
Oh no, he's Muslim
Well, now standards, I'm bending
Expectations shifting
And if then -
I never heard a recollection
Or thoughts of his future and
Did he want children?
Or perhaps I was afraid
To ask questions
'Cuz I didn't want to hear answers
I'd rather just feel good
About all the things of him
I misunderstood.
But tonight, heh -
I'm picketing white fences
And storybook princes
And dreams of Sleeping Beauties
and apples and
Belle's balls

And my glass slipper -
Return it all!
'Cuz my fairytale fantasies
Were taking me for a ride-
And years went by,
Three to be exact.
And perhaps...
Well, matter of fact ---
I was caught up in the lie.
The lie of thinking this average guy
Was somehow my -
Prince Charming
So darling!
Stop yawning,
And shake off this dream-
'Cuz a pumpkin is a pumpkin
Not a chariot, as it seems.
And a man isn't a mouse
And if you a beauty,
He might be a beast
To say the least.
And you can kiss and you kiss
But you won't ever flip that frog.

Into this —
Chocolate man
That has chocolate hands
And lives on some distance land

So tonight, I'm raisin' my right hand,

Solemnly swearing

Instead of crying' out why me, Lord why -- instead,

I'll change my habit

Because faith in God

Without realistic works is dead

Winterized

You looked sweet to me, uncertain of when you
turned to bitter.
I felt summer around you, but now, all I'm getting is
winter.
And it's cold.
Come over here, and warm me up.
Like a hot cup
of tea.
Stir a little bit of you inside
To remind me of what you were.
I call you sweet, so there's no need for honey or
sugar.
Sugar, come back to me.
The way we were introduced.
'Cuz it's already dropping temperature
outside these walls, so with you --
I can't get use.
To long cold nights and short days

of a kidnapped sun's rays,
I'm amazed at how quickly this axis has turned
Wish instead of you making me get shivers,
Once again, you'd make me burn.

Numb Love
A Tanka

I became numb to
love from you. Like winter's cold
on my skin. You sting
my heart deep within. Alas -
Spring comes to melt pain away.

My Heart Waits For You

My heart has been secretly waiting for you.

Unbeknownst to me, it aches for you.

Eagerly sits inside a glass bottle like a long lost message

Waiting to saddle and ride full throttle upon a white stallion with you,

In hopes you will gallop back passed our past to me --- charmingly

and rescue our once felt love.

It waits for you.

Operates separate from my body and mind and all this time that's passed

Alas, like a shore crashing against the sand, it's smacked me with its hand,

demanding my attention to tell me

That it waits for you.

And when you tell it you love it.

It believes you.

Funny, I don't. But it does.

Pours blood in remembrance of what once was.

Hearing love sounds different coming from your lips than when it drips from any other.

Even when I can't stand it, my heart, it ... it waits for you.

Waits in the cold, so I put it on hold ... chilled on ice twice to preserve lonely nights.

Where fights were scarce, and we once created love.

And so, my heart has been secretly waiting for you.

Unbeknownst to me, it aches for you.

Beats for you erratically, in staccato,
like a locator wanting to locate you ---
your pulse.
Restore what is now lost.

But, I go on living, function perfectly, pretending that life is fine

Pleading that love is blind, and that is how I operated when you were mine.

But, while I'm living and giving; growing, my heart knows

That it is secretly waiting for you.

It has stolen away countless days of secret rendezvous with yours in an attempt to betray us.

My heart has become my Judas.

Deceiving my mind and spirit's trust.

Leaving me with what remains of the pains of life's reality mixed with my skewed, unspoken fallacy

That is to explain why, at best, we're estranged -- purposely forced strangers,

Preventing the danger of falling too deeply, blindly, open-heart-and-mindedly into the depths of our love.

Though my heart waits there.

Unwavered, unchanged or moved by the complexities of reason or changing seasons.

Awaits anxiously with a protruding hole carved from your heart's key,

Waiting for you to ride on a white unicorn stallion of chivalry

and unlock our long awaited destiny.

Deep down underground beneath the
confounds of life's rounds
Torn, tattered, shattered and battered
But still beating with both purpose
and reason,
It waits for you.

Chapter 5

REBIRTH

It can be quite a humbling experience to take a long, hard, unbiased look in the mirror and realize that you need to change. To realize that there are some things and habits about yourself that are detrimental to your positive state of being – albeit it spiritually, mentally, emotionally or physically. You have two options. You could ignore it, and continue down a mild or drastic destructive path, or you can decide it is time to dig deep, make some hard change, and realize YOU ARE WORTH SAVING.

I'm certain we all go through a pseudo rebirth of who we are and what our purpose is at some stage in life. I encountered mine in my mid-twenties. I retract that last line. I'm still in the process of my rebirth. I've changed. Transformed. I began to truly understand who I was and embrace and accept myself for who I was, flaws and all, unapologetically. It was painful, and it still is …as I encounter growing pains, but it is well worth it. I encourage you, quickly BECOME who you were designed to be. The sooner you let go of all life's semantics and arrive into your purpose, the happier you will be. There will be growing pains, a period of purging of things and people and love lost along the way, but the nearing to the light at the end of the tunnel is well-worth it. I anxiously await the celebration of new birthdays in this transformed figurative sense of who I've become. I am not ashamed of my history, patient with my present and exhilarated about the future. I understand this woman. I like this woman. I love this woman! She is me. I get to know her more intimately every day as I watch me become who I am purposed to be. If you're currently lost … I offer this chapter as a life jacket to you. It's okay to put other people and things to the side, and realize you are precious and worth a fulfilled life.

Balancing Act

Ready, set, time to begin
Cameras rollin'
Flash, lights and action
Balancing
Life all on one tippy toe
No time for pacing
Only time to go!
Tight rope
Aspiring hope
Reach for the stars
Go and grab Mars
All the while
Treading water, don't choke
No room for drowning
There's success to provoke
Don't break this
While juggling that
Make room for more
Enter many hats.

Twist me

Bend me

Pull me

Spin me

In different directions

Split me into sections

Testing

Testing

Thirst after the key

Question is

What will your boiling point be

Past 212 Fahrenheit degrees

Will you crack under pressure?

No pressure

But time

More pressure

Less time

Your life's

A constant race

To the finishing line

Balancing act

There's success to begat

Abra Cadabra

Now pull that out your hat.

Retire To Bed

Eyes heavy hovered by lids that lower to hurry them
to tomorrow's day.
Vision blurries as the present scurries to throw
yesterday away.
Tomorrow's creeping as today's sorrows are weeping
'round the dawns decay.

Blurry Vision

I woke up
Amid an aftermath of a self-afflicted aquatic bath--
that I had drawn.
I was the culprit and the cause.
Pause.
Eyes inflated and swollen shut.
The result of a bed full of cries.
Tears dried on pillowcase.
After trickling down the terrain of a tattered face.
I don't often visit this place.
But, here I am, strewn 'cross my bedding.
In need of some shedding.
Need of some cleansing.

In need of a peeling --- my aching soul needed some healing.

So, I self-medicated and pried it out.
Cried it out.

From the top of my lungs while my tear ducts wet it out.
Overly exhausted with an inability to jump, yell and
shout.
Yes, even I self-wallow, pity-party swallow
Occasionally.
It's therapeutic, and I've conjured my own form of
therapy.
There's no one better than me, to medicate me.

Morning Shower

I lack motive.

Breathless but still breathing.

Clueless as to the root of the reason, yet -

Disconnected from purpose and passion.

In a state, better yet a country, of melancholy.

So, I submerged self in a bath full of you

I, the main ingredient in an island of your soup.

Marinade me with your nutrients so that I

may dangle on a cliff, hanging somewhere

between heaven and ecstasy.

We started silently, in the dark.

I wasn't ready to be exposed.

In awe of how your wet heat beat on me.

Like the first rain to intermingle with the sand

particles upon the Sahara.

My skin soaked you in ... it called you by name.

I lay my face flat against the cold tile, and close my
pupils -
that roll into the back of my being
in an effort to have one less sense blocked by this
feeling,
of suspension between last and now.
You have my mental twisted in a dow--ry, that I owe to
you.
You are the extension of me.
So lift, catapult and take me higher - make me flyer
than the normalcy of this present reality.
Parade down on me like a tropical rain.
Storm, shatter, pitter-patter, clash and clatter on me.
Conjure the rise and fall of the ocean upon my back.
Revitalize the effervescence that I've seemed to lack
I begin to feel energy pulsating violently on my skin,
Invigorating and penetrating in -
an attempt to pierce my soul.
Create in me, a whole.
You run like a river along the terrain down the hair
follicles of my mane.
Dripping off the ends like a faulty faucet.
Don't end yet.
This is soothing.

I breathe you in.

The steam dances upward toward my cortex.

I tingle.

Intensely overwhelming. Overwhelm me.

From head to toe, I succumb to your invitation to
envelope me.

Wrap me aquatically in your hydraulic essence.

I want to tattoo your presence.

I turn the dial hotter in an effort to barely stand you.

Challenging you to intensify your present alibi.

*Dry the melancholy out of me ... off
of me...*

*and rinse it counterclockwise down the
drain into an abyss.*

That, I'll write but never re-visit.

Melancholy, you'll be missed.

Oh, the ritual of my morning showers.

Ease my pain, and revitalize my power.

Solitude

In need to retreat away from life for a little while
Nothing's really wrong, just need new reasons to
bring smiles
On to my face
To re-appreciate my place
My space
In this life.
His grace
My life's plight.
To recenter
To reshape
To readjust
To reaffirm.
I won't go too far or be gone too long.
I'll be back before you can listen
to a mind full of your favorite songs.
You can find me
somewhere not far from the sea.
So that I can see

my reflection in the blue water.
'Cuz the water never troubled me.
Plus, there's crisp, fresh air
Not too much of a care -
In the world.
Just as long as the waves crash
and 'round the moon we twirl.
I won't take my laptop or even the cell
won't alarm the loved ones -
won't ring a bell
May take a good book and of course, pen and pad
to reflect upon life
and the memories I've had.
Taking note on where I'm going.
Challenge the harvest I'm sowing.
On the search for peace, tranquility and ease
not up for much conversation
let me alone now, please.

I just need to breathe

Become a stranger in another's shoes
be the tourist of another place
Get over my own blues.
I'll be back
once I've revitalized my self muse

don't look for a transformation
No revelation nor new news.
Just nod and smile, acknowledging my return
No smoke signals -
I'll write what I've learned.

Cocoon

I checked in a stranger.
In a different city
Tattered clothes and unwashed skin.
In need of a vacation within.
Hoodie on.
Words were minimal.
I just wanted my room.
To tuck and hide away from the world.
To shelter myself from myself.
I wanted to be silent.
Because I was feeling so alive inside --- I
Needed to quiet the noises of life that surrounded me
From around me
So that I could hear what I was trying to tell myself.
It was a secret.
This was Room 101.
The place where my thoughts could become loud.
They were screaming for my attention,

But I was so caught up in the
dimensions of the world
That I couldn't hear myself loud enough
So, I allowed myself –
to need this.
To take the time to breathe this.
To contemplate, write and then,
read this.

Didn't even know I needed ---
to drive down I-95 and
hit pavement and pound
to drown out the sounds
Of life.
The diverged road where asylum and hermit meet.
To get off my feet.
To quest ... to seek,
To hunger and eat of myself.
I was in need of company with myself.
By myself ---- silently.
Privately.

No longer could I lie to me.

The irony in how loud silence can be.

My insides were feeling too alive for me!

I was erupting

I could feel the lava boiling inside of me.

So, I trekked South, down I-95 to drive into the depths
of my soul.

I left a caterpillar and became a butterfly - WHOLE.

I drove down 95 in search of a cocoon to transform
myself.

Find the time to nestle one's self.

To self-develop myself.

This hotel room enveloped me.

I wasn't even ready for self.

I didn't check out 'til I grew tired of self.

For Dark Shall Come
A Triolet

For dark shall come and new day bring
A renewed attempt at life's trials.
Leap I, at sound of birds chirping
For dark shall come and new day bring
Mourn not at moon that's descending
Or dawn's sun rays awakening
For dark shall come and new day bring
A renewed attempt at life's trials.

Perseverance

One small step forward for three large steps back
Like I'm dodging monkeys from climbing on my back
A constant struggle of picking up perpetual slack,
But I got this determination to stay on track
My hopes and dreams are washed away by the rain
The inequities of life continuously drive me insane
I attempt to remain faithful and insight I gain,
But the hardships of life keep me in the passenger's
lane
Frozen in the starting block, left to lose its race
Fronting with a positive disposition, façade and smile
on face
The frustrations of longing to be successful in haste
Suffocating by the familiar walls of this mentally
enslaved place
The agony of complacency, always defending my
case,
But I move forward

Slowly and surely
Never looking back
Pressing on.

Utter Determination
A Triolet

I dangle
distinctly
down the
depths of
destiny
daring it to
deceive me.
Deciding that
doubt wouldn't
dance in
destiny's way but
dwindle
disillusioned
down a
dune, dying.
I dangled
dynamically

down the

direction of my

destiny.

Dangled defiantly determined.

By The Horns
A Quinzaine

Life is what you make of it.
What have you made it?
What will you?

Go With the Flow

Fall leaves came in exchange to a once budding tree;
I watched it while mixing lemons with my half glass
of tea,
As an approaching freight ship through the morning
fog nears
To the thrills from a reluctant sparrow I hear.
The sun captured a snowman today
In an attempt to spring for a brighter day.
It caused the tickling of fresh lavender to my nose
While two daffodils droop from underneath the
window
That I hop scotched by to reach the willow tree
That helps me wrap a worn scarf 'round me;
And pull winter boots up above the bending of my
knee.
The moon chased me in the house earlier than
expected
from playing with a caterpillar I captured from being

neglected

Which caused grass blades to leap through the gaping
of my feet

In hopes this hawk gifts them a melting pot of more
than just sleet.

I sleep best, rest, to the rhythms of afternoon rain

By opening my senses to sense about change.

It is inevitable, nothing's ever weatherproof.

Just ask the gapping leak atop my momma's tin roof.

So what if not carrying an umbrella amid storm proves
insane

'Less you appreciate the effects of singing in the rain.

Moments of Life

I have moments to catch.

Yes, hopelessly romantic dreams to fetch.

Stagnant air to breath.

A man whose chest to rest I need.

A mind to feed.

There's a tear somewhere in me ---

that's yet to shed.

That's yet to trickle down a face

that has smiles left to give.

I've got LIFE left to live.

A vow to take

A child to make

A stretched hand waiting for a completed handshake.

I've yet to feel the earth shatter or shake.

For Heaven's sake!

There's a poem brewing inside of me.

A warm cup of honeyed herbal tea.

Autumn's leaves to rake

The sun and its rays to wake.

I saw a lost soul I'd longed to save

An experience I've an appetite to crave.

An imprisoned moment trialed to be free.

A problem to be solved within me.

I've got moments to catch!

Dreams to fetch!

A wave to ride

Unjust laws to abide

A long-term goal left to strive — for

There's beauty to adore

The essence of an enigma'd core

A can to place within a cabinet to store

A book that's not written

An enemy left to be forgiven

Sin to repent

A dollar waiting to be spent

I've a star to gaze and wish on

An adventure to spawn

Yes, I've got moments to catch.

Memories of life left to fetch.

Self-Acceptance

I finally decided to accept myself today

So, I put the makeup away

And pulled out the weave

I just got naked, then breathed -

And looked at me from all angles

Lots of flaws and insecurities

Made myself take a slow 360 degree

I finally decided to accept myself today

Found a drawer so I could put the mask away

And now, what can I say?

I'm left vulnerable, as I gaze at my lack of disguise

The extra fat that wraps around my stomach and thighs

The little mark that nests below my left eye

I guess by now, it's time I realized, I -

Will never be a shade or two lighter

Or adorn eyes the shades of nature's hues or brighter

My hair won't ever resemble Rapunzel's

And my dialect will always detect -
A mix of suburban and hood jumble.
I finally decided to accept myself today
In all of my size 24 glory
Sit back and relax
This is my story.

I Was Too Human
A Monorhyme

I was too Hip Hop for him
Too turn the bass up in my ride and let that 808
knock for them
I could quote too much Tupac for him
Too, it was all a dream, Biggie Smalls mixed with a
Lil' Kim for them
I was too sweatpants and flip flop for him
I was too bourgeoisie for them
Too dangled pearls with my 4 1/2 inch and cardigan
He said I was too intelligent
Too Lauryn Hill ... misunderstood for my own good ---
for him
I was too deep for them
Crooning Jill Scott, Don't You Remember Me at him
I was too Christian
Didn't sex or cuss enough to entice him with trim
I was too much for them

Too loud and boisterous, big and proud, overflowing my
brim
I was too around the way for them
Bi-social economically mixed with 'burbs and city grim
Too free-spirited and daring, going out on a limb for them
I'd wouldn't tote the glock, circle the block for him
While writing poetic rhymes out of the whim
I was too crazy, sexy, cool for them
Too calculated with my financial situation
I had been given too much passion
I was too much a rebel with a cause for them
Too wise to his surprise so it'd be our demise for him
Told me I was too perfect for them
Too righteous with morals, proper and prim
I was too Hip Hop for him.
I told them I was just too human.

Intellectual Fiend

A student of the mind
Thoughts delve deep into the sublime
Concepts race from forward and behind
She lives in academia; an intellect
Rather tread deeply in cogitation complex
Than wade in a shallow illiterate nation
Gets off cerebrally on mental stimulation
Desires to expand the parameters of reason
Yearns to progress knowledge with every turned
season.
A hunger that keeps on feeding.
A mental acute; metastasis through bleeding
Knowledge to the cerebral cortex of the brain
In the grooves of her sulci consciousness remains
Subjecting her thought to development and
manipulation
Finds freedom in understanding; philosophical
liberation
Absorbing information to mind is essential

Equates intelligence as a powerful credential

In love with the mental identity of self

Through psyche, she attributes boundaries of internal
wealth

Capacity of erudition churns like a machine

Covets the process of thought; an intellectual fiend.

Muted Swan

She's afraid.

Afraid that

How her words are conveyed when laid skillfully

'cross the lines on a page

They won't necessarily adequately behave when

spoken.

So, she retracts back to her den.

Back to her laptop

Back to this pen.   Her safe haven.

Where no one can judge her for her words.

Where folks are unable to ridicule her verbs.

See, there's a difference between poetry and spoken

word.

The pen doesn't stare back.

People do.

The pad doesn't overreact.

People do.

Poetry doesn't counterattack.

People do.

Hell, even you're judging her for the absurdity of writing this, too.

So, she retracts back to her den.

Yup, back to her laptop.

Back to her friend. The pen.

It has become her safe haven.

Her dirty little secret that at one point, nobody ever knew.

Her self-medicated crutch that just helped take off the edge.

Helped her manage to keep her head --- above water.

Poetry never interrupted her flow.

Never told her, "Yea ... yea, yea, yea ! already knew."

It was a silenced friend.

A means to an end.

It was a neutral atmosphere where mental perplexities mix with emotional complexity and would create---

Well, would create a sacred trust and understanding.

She's not too convinced that spectators understand.

So, she won't verbalize.

Won't even dare to memorize.

For that is her crutch for why she can't possibly amplify her poetic rhetoric.

In front of a crowd? With her words? --- FORGET it.

Self-convinced herself that folks just wouldn't get it.

She'd regret it.

Wouldn't they just rather READ poetry anyway?

She wallows: Why won't the world rather READ written poetry --- forgo, the experience.

She's yet to conceptualize it all to make logical sense.

So, she struggled … struggles

To take what's been simmering 'round the compartments of her mental profound

And add a voice to them.

This is her ode.

Her ode to a muted susan.

A muted susan with a burning heart and a fleeting storm

Of written words that never are given an ability to speak.

An ability to reach.
Never have tone, never influx or
weep.
Its sounds won't ever bounce 'round and
off what sounds lounge walls.
Won't ever grow grandeur, grow rich
nor tall.

She settles for poetry
And retracts back to her pen
Yes, back to her laptop.
And back to her den. It's her safe haven.
She nestles there.
Wrestles with words that find recluse there.
Prophetic passages that'll never be heard.
Never be ministered
Never anoint into spoken word.
All because she retracts back to her pen.
Back to her laptop.
Back to poetry, her friend.
Until the time when ---

SHE GETS OVER HERSELF
and believe me
that time is nearing.

Reversed Samson

Looking in the mirror the reflection portrayed

A misconstrued view of American beauty

I no longer wanted to aspire to be this falsified, yet

glorified image of Barbie

'Cuz she don't got no hips or natural tits

Nor a natural jiggle in her thighs or stomach

And I could no longer stomach - my constant battle

to see her

The desire to want to be her

My internal composition didn't "make-up" her.

She was too tight, too rigid, too cookie-cutting

defined

and well, I'm a sista, I came out the womb with hips,

thighs and a behind.

I wanted the world to be drawn pass it and to my

mind

therefore, striving to fit into the mold was not

profiting my bottom line.

So, I decided to redefine my vision

of beauty.

It started with my hair.

She was becoming uneventful, so I had to cut her loose.

Packed her bags and sent her out of town on the
quickest caboose.

She'd suffered long enough amid the products, the
perms, the heat and hygienic abuse.

My hair tresses felt something like a tight noose

That was suffocating my head

So, I quit processing and chopped it all off instead

And for the first time ever, I saw the real, unaltered
version of me –

Chemically – free.

This was the making of my history.

Picture me.

Feeling completely and wholeheartedly –

Naked

The first time I vacated my premises and ventured
outside,

Insecure with my decisions, it felt like a thousand eyes,
were staring at the nape of my neck, upset with my
decision.

There was no longer a division
between the world and my hair.
Thoughts racing, heart pacing,
I had reinvented myself to this big ol' world I was facing.
Words can't describe how equally dead and
simultaneously alive I felt.
I had finally accomplished this gigantic task and placed
it under my belt.
The days went from hesitation to ultimate exhilaration.
I felt alive.
I was ready to thrive.
I wanted to just dive-
Head first into a pool or sea or walk vicariously in the
midst of a rainstorm.
My statement, to show the world I'm above the norm
Just simply because I could.
All these years I felt misunderstood.
Somehow, my natural hair better correlated with me
it fit like glue, who would'a knew
that through a simple task of shearing tresses for all to
see,

I'd be cutting away at the layers and
freeing me.

Nefertitian Metaphor

Jewels implanted deep in the bellies of the Earth
decorate my exterior.

My breasts shaped the hills of the Judean desert.

My inner thighs concave the topography of the Sinai
Peninsula.

My chocolate complexion spills into Côte d'Ivoire
cocoa beans.

My widespread hips like two half crescent moons
that light the African sky.

Bright as Sirus of the Canis Major are my eyes.

My tears fall like diamonds across the Botswanan
jwaneng mine.

Grace transcends from the vertebrae of my spine.

My smile, the richest gold found in Zimbabwe.

The mold broke after my exquisiteness was sculpted
from clay.

I am the definition of beauty.

I cleanse in the Mediterranean Sea.

Thunder is my laughter amid a Malavian storm.

An heir from greatness, from royalty I was born.

The African djembe drum is my rhythm.

My eyes are found off the Chilean coast, black Obsidian.

My skin, smoother than silk weaved in Madagascar.

My spirit, brought life to an Acoustic guitar.

My neck, the strong foundation that supports my mind.

My essence has weaved in and out of life's time.

I am divine.

I made manifest from the mouth of the Almighty and the
rib of he.

I am she.

Earth's mother.

His lover.

Beauty is in admiration of me.

My Great Walls of China are sweeter than fresh dripping
honey from the womb of a bee

my posterior, a soft Cumulus cloud after the rain.

The lions of the Sahara admire my mane.

My nipples, like black Tahitian pearls washed upon the
shore.

REBIRTH

My love, patient, kind and endures.

My navel, a deep abyss that reconnects the world back to its Inner core.

My body scent lies on the petals of a rose
Copper descends from the nostrils of my nose.

My menstrual bleeds rubies that seed Tanzania
I am the patent, the offspring of His idea
my hands crafted the Egyptian Pyramids.

My vocal chords' vibrations brought forth sound and language.

My blink is an eclipse.

Death and life flow from the power of my lips.

My bowels fertilized some seven nations.

I am the uniMother of all civilization.

My thighs divide like the Red Sea and gave birth to complete humanity.

My strength, courage and wisdom are Plato and Socrates' anomaly.

My intellect discovered Hieroglyphics and Arithmetic.

I hone an inexplicable "Je ne se qua," diplomacy and classiness.

My mind, Daedalus' Labyrinth, amazing and defined
my biological clock created life, love and time.

Chapter 6

DEAR GOD

ear God, you are all I ever need and all I ever want in this world. My life is yours wholeheartedly. I apologize in advance for times when I am an utter disappointment to you and pray that between you, your Son and the Holy Spirit that resides inside of me that I make you elated more days than not. I work consciously daily to kill my flesh and become a better child to you. Thank you for loving me unconditionally, even when I didn't know how to love myself at all. You are my sole existence, and I pray to know you, understand you and be in your presence more now than I have ever desired in my entire life. Life is hard and I'd be a fool to ever think I could do it alone, without you. I need you more than I need life itself. I am so honored to progressively know you on a deeper level. I am in awe of your power, your love, your mercy and your grace every day. I give my gift of wordsmith to you. The moment I lose sight of that and you, take it away. Thank you for never letting go of me. I am indefinitely grateful.

Mourning Newspaper

The news bothers me,

Annoyed with broadcasters that lie to me,

Telling stories of a desperate society,

As if there's no Savior -- no high deity,

Equipped with a message strong enough to rid the anxiety,

Of this helled world.

The news bothers me,

Conveying grimed tales of various variety,

From catastrophic natural calamities to naive notoriety,

As if there's no Savior ---

no high deity,

Risen with the ability to cut the excess and bring about sobriety,

To this helled world.

DEAR GOD

The news bothers me,
I'm certain it must be lying to me,
I know a God that is crying out to we,
Disheartened with our inability to draw nigh to he,
As if he's no Savior --- no high deity,
As if he lacks grace, lacks power, lacks mercy to
decree,
A lost soul be transformed and renewed to flee,
From this helled world.

The news bothers me,
It whispers the opposite of what I know my Father to be,
Glorifying the work of a cunning enemy,
When I know a God who holds a master key,
Who created a gospel that is the Word for free,
Who is the Alpha, the Omega and the Creator of the
agape love I see,
Each time I disregard the news and by faith, I believe,
By faith I cleave,
By faith I receive,
Because of faith, I can reprieve --
The problem is faith without works is DEAD as can be,
Dead as the victim I'm left victimized to see,
Each time I catch a glimpse of this news that keeps
bothering me.

Best Selling Bibliography

Mark my word.

Since the Genesis there was a

Revelation of who he was.

Even if the Numbers would lie,

His miraculous Exodus back in Matthew

Was a testament that he is the tRuth.

Judges would even vouch for that.

The daily Chronicles of life will scribe his Acts.

His spirit is heard in any sung Psalms

Wisdom witnessed in any written Proverbs.

He can take anything Lukewarm and make it hot.

His autobiography tops any best-selling book you got.

With him, there's no need for Lamentations

Any grief or pain, he fixes with supernatural

restoration.

He is the word.

and the word alone.

Plus, he's got the Titus Job in the entire world.

King of all Kings.

Casual Chat with God

There are a lot of things I'm uncertain of.
My townhome could crumble from the very cemented
foundation to the rooftop lying above.
My job could go in shambles, and I tumble from this
prestige position to pools of poverty,
And this nation's sovereignty is slim and bleak at
minimum, to say the least
Life can be quite the beast
It's hard to progress to a mortgage from the cycles
of a lease
This leash that always pulls you back into this
cesspool of stuff might happen.
You're never fully the captain
of your own fate.
You'll always experience equal ebbs of less if it flows
too great
Things will infuriate
you

they will aggravate

you

But you, God,

you never do.

And you

you never leave.

And for that

I thank you.

The one constant in my life.

That's never changing, always standing, never

demanding of me.

Just accepting of me.

Meeting me where I am.

Where I stand.

Even where I fall short

of your glory.

You are ALWAYS there.

I'm in awe of your story.

You never cease to amaze me

with all that you do

All that you know.

Never staccato.

Always connected.

Always present.

I reverence - your presence.

Transformation

I tried to fill His void
with earthly things,
but then I got filled with Him
Transformed.
He's the complete recipe
for your spiritual hunger
I always knew him
wish I had just kept him 'round
like when I was younger.
Picture me, Sunday morning,
hung over in bed
Scantily-clad the night before
in the club
Instead of in church getting fed.
Not a care in the world
I was
spiraling out of control
Enter the Lord
He stretched out His hand

and spared my lost soul.
You can call it a rebirth
Call it whatever you like
Because this new itch I got
Leaves me seeking Him
every night.
Never understood why
I kept failing life's test
Then I realized,
God's my answer-key,
and I'm His very best.
Now, it is I
who'd rather ride
Passenger side
The Heavenly Father and I.
And I
Rather Be
Set free
spiritually
Kill my flesh, feed the soul
Let the Spirit take control.

Didn't you know
His yoke is easy?

And His burden's so light

God's got me feeling just right.

Righteousness, I'm granted

His seed has been planted

When I think about

His glory, I just

Lose it

I want you to choose it!

Turn from your sin,

and then

Embrace a whole lot of him.

Sit back, relax and

just watch how he moves

Tell me, when the end is here

which path will you choose?

The Alpha and Omega will transform

Stuff right up on the inside of you.

Why not just let him be

all that you need?

I'll rep him harder

Than I rep my degree or this deed.

Lord, fill the nonbeliever

with your word is my plea.

This little light of mine,

I'm going to let it shine
and brand me God's bling bling,
now rock him on your ring.
Throw him on your wheels
Let him cop your mil'
Jehovah can provide your deal.
This isn't no fad
this is my reality show
We walking round this piece
Like its Jericho
You know!
Trendsetting
We Reppin'
Jesus Christ
For our life.
Now let that be the standard
Let Him throw your hands up
In Total praise
I vow to rep him all of my days.
Isn't no questions about it
I'm blessed, no stressing 'bout it
My God,
I've finally found
The true meaning of life

His will,

Eternal salvation

Reaching souls

This is my plight.

And I

Use to think

I was

such a grown woman in this world

now I

realize,

all along,

I was just His little girl.

Worshipper In Me

There's a worshipper in me
quite different than many.
It's not often through text or words
that God speaks to me.
But, I feel him closest
through the harmony
of the timbre.
Through the intricate scales
of the piano keys.
Through the changes in tone -
in sweet harmony.
When I need to speak to God,
I don't always get on my knees.
I take off my veil,
and I dance for thee.
Through song, not words,
he and I speak
through performance and praise,

my afflictions are set free.
Not often do I
Come to the altar for rest,
But I know God understands
my heart's desire
When I sauté arabesque
or pirouette.
I usher in the Holy Spirit
by connecting my emotions,
spirit and desires through step.
Up all night, in the midst of storm,
I dance 'til there's nothing left.
Of me
'til my rhythmic prayer is
sealed and received
No words spoken, only moves
through hand, body and feet.
'Til my physical is left weak.
Through song and motion
I hear Him speak.
At times, it's the same song
left on repeat.
I turn, I bend, I arch - to the heaven's,
I reach.

No words can truly define
what my soul needs
through interpretation of
dance, I state my plea.
To the sky
Tear in eye
God why -
Out of breath
Nothing left
But faith, hope and trust
At times, replaced by prayer
I know, my dance, - still
availeth much.

Jehovah Shalom

You gave me your peace,

And it's funny

Because although it is written,

I never asked for that level of contentment.

An internal commitment.

Peace.

I never knew you as peace

Even though you blessed it to all that

Obey your commandments

But, I never knew you as peace

Not a peace that passes all understanding

Not a peace in the midnight hour

Not a peace be still

Not peace to dry my tears

Peace to coddle my fears

I never knew you as peace

Called on you as many other things

My Father

My Strength

My Wisdom

My Helper

My Healer

My Deliverer

Alpha and Omega

The Great I am

The author and finisher

And even if I knew you,

I never received you

By faith in this manner.

Thought I had to go at it all alone.

And if by faith I receive

Then by faith I must believe

That you are peace.

And I, to be a peacemaker.

Leaving trails of peace

As I come and go

Gracefully to and fro.

Not happiness or

A glimpse of joy

But an inner peace.

Calm

A still

An unwavering

DEAR GOD

An everlasting
Stream of peace
That coats my spirit,
Wraps my soul
And submerges my mind
In peace.
I never knew you as peace.
As a kept perfect peace.
Peace that covers worry.
So, why do I worry?
Peace that covers stress
Confusion and
A disillusioned sense.
Why do I wonder?
You ARE Jehovah Shalom.
My peace.
My peace as I rise
My peace as I fall
Your PEACE
Shall reside still in the midst
Of it all.
You GAVE it to me
This sweet, supernatural
Peace

I pray for your peace

Of mind, peace of spirit

Peace of my body

Lord, a sweet piece

Of your peace

That I can devour

Forever showering in.

Thank you for the peace.

Take the rest of it all away

May it drift at bay

And just leave me with

Your precious, perfect peace.

Sun

I was empty.

Vacant of a sense of who owned me.

Had become known to be

Fragmentally strewn about the corners of life

recklessly

Somewhere in an abyss

Wrapped in tainted,

Tattered clothes as my blanket.

A stranger to who I had become.

Far removed from the One.

I managed to lift my weary countenance in direction

of a beaconing Sun

That was relentless on resiliently cleaving my soul.

He desired to create within me a new whole.

I retreated.

Gripped by self-penitence, fearful of habitually

becoming defeated,

'Til the day I awakened, an inhabitant of this abyss

no more and conceded.

To him, I pleaded.
Mustered up enough humility, 'til pride
and it depleted
Promised him he was all that I ever
wanted and needed.

That without him, I'd continue to go through this world
defeated.

... And he answered.

Out of his sunrays, he poured out enough sunny days

To bring about restoration to my life's haze.

His healing took away pain.

Provided enough sunlight to counteract the mere
thought of rain.

Beamed hope into me.

'Til it pulled out what I was destined to be.

He transformed me drastically.

Turned my woes into gold.

Made within me a new whole.

So, now we dance ---

We dance daily --- gracefully to the sunrise and set of his

purpose.

Strengthening me.

Providing me

With enough agility

To become who I was destined to be ----through Him.

And him alone.

I Surrender All

Father,

If it weren't for you,

I'd be dead a long time ago,

And I'm writing you this letter

Just to let you know

How much I need you, once again,

As I deal with life's tests

The devil is so busy,

And he's doing his very best

To attack me

Mentally and emotionally

And yay, thou I walk through this valley

Of death

I sometimes fear his evil

Are you with me?

When I don't have the strength

In me

To see the end of this valley,

DEAR GOD

I turn and desire to lean on you

To keep me standing

To keep me demanding

Better from me

Better from this world

I'll always attest to the fact that

I'm still a little girl

spiritually,

Trying to grasp a hold on life

trying to live right

It seems like the enemy is causing my strife

Each battle, an ongoing fight,

And truth be told,

I know I'm not always doing what's right

Not always praying each night

Sometimes, my spirit feels a lil' lukewarm

And Lord, answer me this, is that the norm?

Been a couple of times where I've wanted you to turn

your back,

Maybe even shut your eye

To the sin I know I've devised

To the way I lived

To the way that I give

Or to the company I chose to keep

Even hearing you tell me

I've sown the harvest that I reap
not to question why blessings seems so bleak.
For some odd reason,
You won't take your hand off my life
No matter what I do,
I can never shake you,
And I know the devil just despises
'Cuz even when I'm lost,
I find a way to draw back nigh to you
I ain't going to lie to you,
I've never been a perfect saint for you
Each day, I wonder if I'm just sliding through
I'd love to take back some of the things that I did
Inside me, there's a light
That just won't stop flickering for you
Won't stop burning for you
Won't let me stumble and die
And why
Lord, have you chosen me out of all
Realizing it's always been a setup
Because my first parents did fall
So this sin is genetically composed in me

Trying hard to correct this history
Spiritually, but I'm wrapped in this flesh,

And it can cause such a mess

One step forward, two steps backward, I confess

I don't want to look hindsight

To find the insight of life

So THIS is MY PLEA

RAIN ON ME

Just pour down all over me

Wholeheartedly

'Cuz I surrender

It all to thee

I fall to my knees

And plead

For thee

something has got a hold on me

The grip is so tight

I choke and can't breathe,

but in my last breath

In my darkest hour,

When my light seems so dim

I feel a warm comfort

And I think

It must be Him,

I cry out to you, dear God,

To help this weakened saint
I once was lost, in that valley,
But this time around,
I yearned to be found
I hear you can move mountains
Read that you part red seas
Heal lepers, feed multitudes
Raise man from the dead,
Make a blind man see
So please, heavenly,
Lead the way,
And guide me through this valley
I know this is the reason
You offered up your son up on Calvary
Carry me, like he
Carried that rugged cross
I'll take the road less traveled by
Like the author Frost
I no longer want to be a pretender
I'm bowing out as a contender
I'm trusting in you
Casting my cares upon you
Got one mustard seed left to give
Heavenly father, teach me to live.

I Found You

I found you
Somewhere between Proverbs and poetry
I found you between Psalms and music.
Heaven and Hell - I found you.
I found you somewhere between pleasure and pain
Love and sex
Sunshine and rain - I found you.
I found you
Between a rock and a soft place.
Humility and disgrace.
Breakfast and dinner.
Through life's losses and learning to become a
winner - I found you.
I found you
Between childhood and now.
I found you between taking a stand and having a fall.
Found you in the midst of it all.
I found you

Somewhere between the stench of midnight air and
judgmental, disapproving stares.
Between childhood divorces and self-inflicted wars - I
found you
Between the alter and adultery.
Hanging between black and white.
Between praying in pews and stumbling out the club at
night.
I found you
Between overachieving and an obsession with
overeating
Between heartache and heartbreak.
Spiritual cravings and promiscuous misbehaving - I found
you.
I found you
Between serenity and chaos.
Between time and now.
Between a tick within a time bomb.
Family feuds and mended friendships.
Through a perm and a nap.
Gospel music and hard core rap - I found you
Between pinching pennies and extra cheese
Between a diploma and a lot of college degrees
Between going into debt and lavish shopping sprees - I

found you

I found you

Between right and wrong

Between the hook and chorus of my favorite song.

Between Alpha and Omega. The block and the bodega.

I found you.

I found you between dreams and reality.

Perfection and fallacy.

Mouth and ear. Courage and fear.

Opaque and transparency.

Righteousness and blasphemy.

I found you between praise and prayer.

The surface and underneath the layer.

I found you.

Between affliction and healing.

The floor and the ceiling.

Between the pages of a novel and the TV.

Weaved in my future and in traces of my history - I found
you.

Amid the popular crowd and walking alone.

On those silent car rides home

 I FOUND you

And it's crazy,

Because YOU NEVER LOST ME

My God!

God, so glad I found You
Between the proverbs of life and my
poetry.

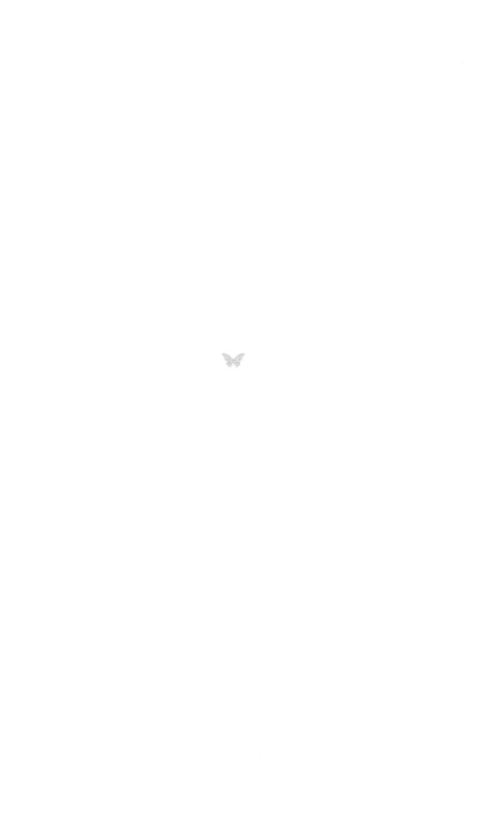

About The Author

Tywanda L. Howie, daughter of James and Marjorie Howie, is a Delaware native and alum of the University of Delaware and Wilmington University where she holds a Bachelor of Arts in English with a concentration in Journalism and a Masters in Business Administration with a discipline in Marketing Management. She currently works in the non-profit industry and as a freelance writer, editor and marketing consultant. Tywanda has a compassion for empowering and motivating others having spent many years mentoring, volunteering in the community and serving on the boards of various organizations.

Tywanda, 29, currently resides at her home in Newark, Delaware and remains active in her church and in the community through speaking, writing and enriching the lives of others. Outside of poetry she enjoys music, the performing arts, philanthropy, laughter and love. To book Tywanda for any upcoming poetry readings, speaking engagements or interviews contact her business manager, Melinda R. Counts at tywandahowie@gmail.com.